LOSE THAT LOSER AND FIND THE RIGHT GUY

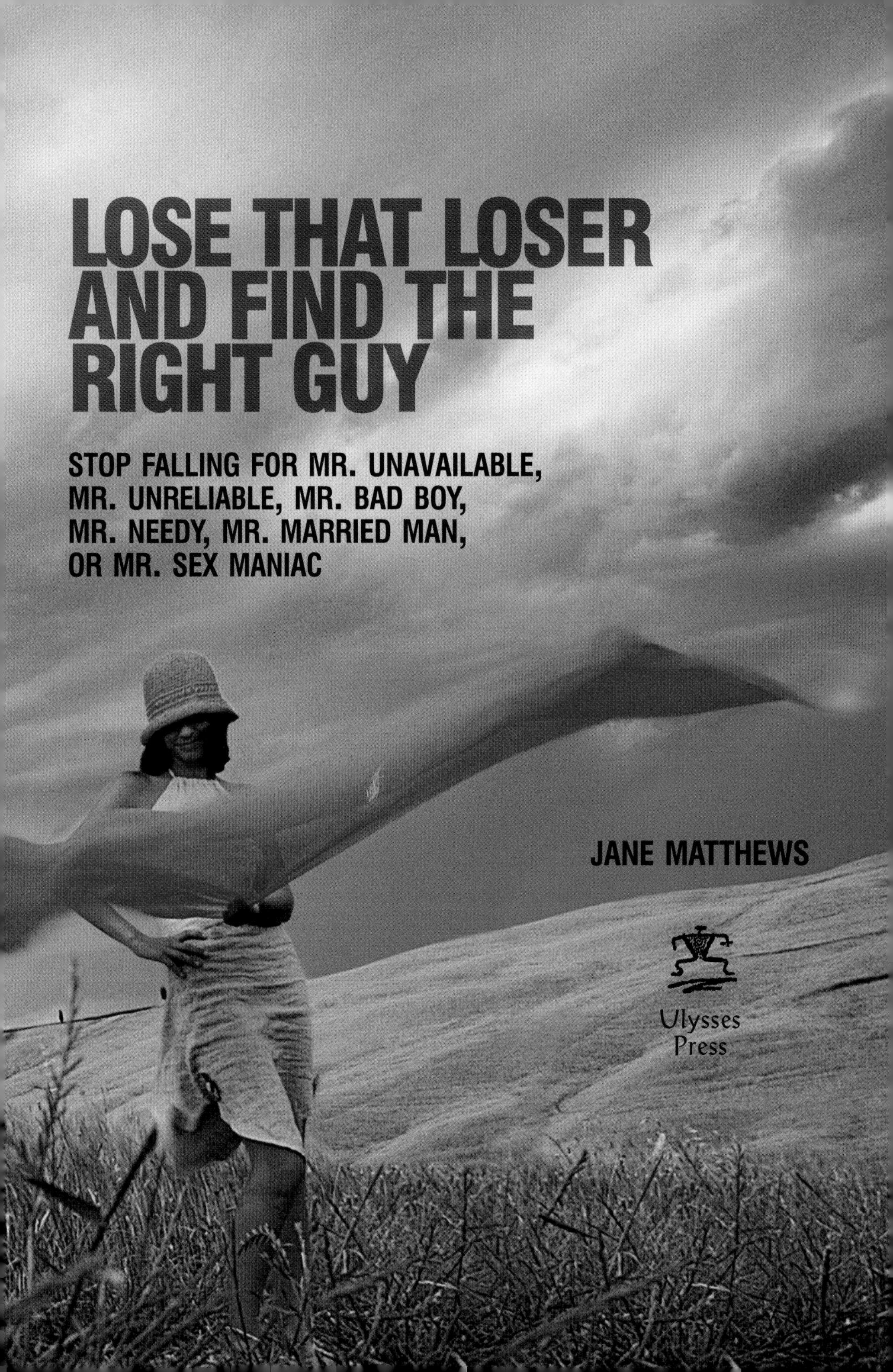

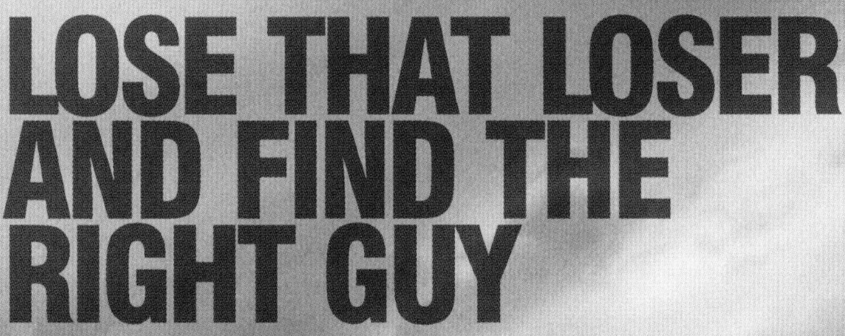

LOSE THAT LOSER AND FIND THE RIGHT GUY

STOP FALLING FOR MR. UNAVAILABLE, MR. UNRELIABLE, MR. BAD BOY, MR. NEEDY, MR. MARRIED MAN, OR MR. SEX MANIAC

JANE MATTHEWS

Ulysses Press

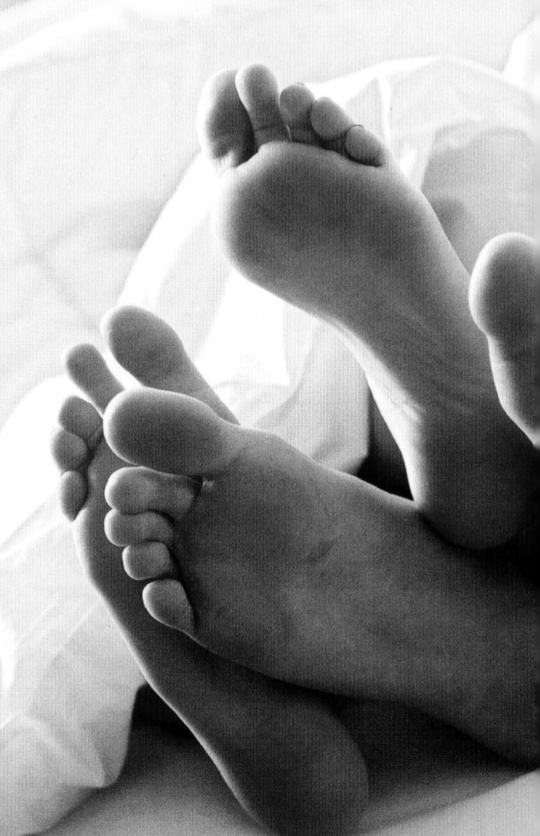

Published in the United States by
Ulysses Press
P.O. Box 3440
Berkeley, CA 94703
www.ulyssespress.com

10 9 8 7 6 5 4 3 2 1

Created and conceived by
Axis Publishing Ltd
8c Accommodation Road
London NW11 8ED
www.axispublishing.co.uk

Library of Congress Control Number
2004110289

ISBN 1-56975-452-7

Creative Director: Siân Keogh
Art Director: Clare Reynolds
Editorial Director: Anne Yelland
Managing Editor: Conor Kilgallon
Production Manager: Toby Reynolds
Production Controller: Jo Ryan

Printed in China

Distributed in the United States by
Publishers Group West

CONTENTS

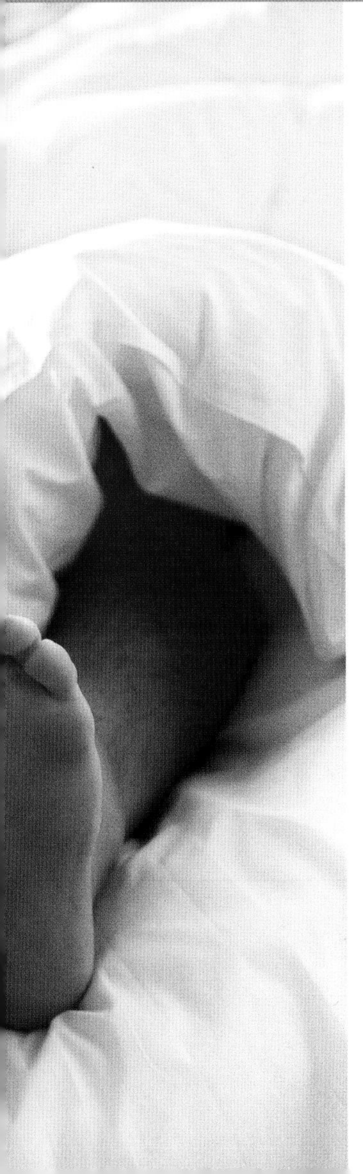

INTRODUCTION

Most of us have had the misfortune of dating a loser at some stage in our life, so know just how painful it can be.

LIFE WITH A LOSER IS GETTING YOU NOWHERE FAST. IT'S TIME TO LIGHTEN UP, BE BOLD, AND MAKE WAY FOR A NEW, BRIGHT FUTURE, UNENCUMBERED BY MR. WRONG

If only the hurt was like a toothache: a visit to the dentist, the bold decision to yank the problem out of your life, and the immense pain is swiftly over. But far more common is the grazed knee scenario: the wound doesn't seem so sore at first so you ignore it, but then it turns septic. Every time you think you're healing, the scab gets knocked and your wound is reinfected. When it finally goes away you are left with a bad scar.

If the title of this book shouted "buy me" as you browsed the shelves, chances are that's because you're sick of your wound and of it hurting so much. You're frightened of the scar it might leave. You look around you and see other people

YOU KNOW HE'S BAD FOR YOU BUT HOW DO YOU LET HIM GO? IT'S NEVER EASY TO KICK A LOSING HABIT. YOU NEED HELP TO MOVE ON, SO KEEP READING...

apparently "getting it right" and wonder why the guys you date always turn out to be losers.

You're probably beginning to wonder whether you have a "pick me" sign over your head, visible only to every guy who's already attached, every commitment-phobe, cling-on, or full-on lothario, every unreliable, unpredictable, unavailable, or plain unpleasant breed of loser.

You want to know how to get your current loser out of your life, and you want to know how you can spot the next one before you allow yourself to fall for him? Fear not. The aim of this book is to help you shake your losing habit for good, so read on...

Starting with a look at some familiar loser types (and the games they play), you'll discover what attracts you to them—and them to you. Once you know and understand what's really pulling your own strings you have a much better chance of rewriting the way you "do" relationships.

The next step is to take a deep breath, think positive thoughts,

YOU DESERVE THE BEST, SO GO ON: TAKE THE DECISION TO GET RID OF YOUR LOSER AND REGAIN CONTROL OF YOUR OWN LIFE AND HAPPINESS

believe in yourself—and your innermost feelings—and rid yourself not only of the loser boyfriend currently making you miserable but also the mindset which, in the past, has encouraged another variety of the same species to come in and simply take his place—like weeds that keep growing back because the roots haven't been pulled out.

We'll also give you tips on how to get through the months that follow the end of your love affair. Unfortunately, the fact that you're in a bad relationship doesn't mean ending it will hurt any less. However, you will then be able to make the most of going solo and—once you're ready—move on to the winner's podium, with the kind of guys who help you feel a whole lot better (not worse) about yourself, and who complement your character, rather than stifling it or criticizing it.

Like any journey, using this book to lose your loser(s) requires you to make a little effort and to challenge yourself as well as your guy. You'll be looking at who you are, what made you that way, what you believe, and what exactly you want in the future.

If that seems like too much hard work, or worries or scares you, just ask yourself whether life with a loser isn't infinitely more effort—and whether you're not more scared of having to put up with your loser for life. Go on, lose that loser…

CHAPTER 1

ARE YOU INTO A LOSER?

It's the easiest thing in the world to spot that your girlfriend's new man is a loser—you know it and so do all your other girlfriends. But spotting that your own new lover is a loser is next to impossible. This chapter is a quickfire guide to some of the more common losers you are likely to encounter in your search for Mr. Right.

PRINCE CHARMING?

You'd have to have been locked in a tower for 100 years, not to know that a girl's gotta kiss a lot of toads before she finds her handsome prince.

THE TROUBLE IS MR. WRONG CAN FEEL LIKE MR. RIGHT IF YOU DON'T HAVE YOUR FLASHING ALERT BUTTON ON AT ALL TIMES

On the whole, toads are pretty easy to spot: they're under your feet, getting in the way, with the other lowlife and it's obvious that getting up close and personal with them will be a poisonous experience.

But what happens when a toad somehow manages to disguise himself as Prince Charming and makes you believe you'll live happily ever after?

Let's face it, we've all been there. Convinced ourselves this love affair really will have a happy ending, only to discover that beneath the shiny exterior he's just another slimeball, expecting you to adore him, warts and all.

Some girls make a real habit of it—take Elena, for example. Stunning girl with bucketloads of talent—and a fatal attraction for any guy whose toothbrush resides at another woman's house. Her men always tell her they'll leave the other woman, but just end up buying a second toothbrush to keep at Elena's place. "In the end I just get tired of having to wake up in the night to let him out and going on vacation by myself," she wails.

Rosie, on the other hand, doesn't stick to one type of toad. Her first partner's love of doing deals bankrupted them, so she then sought security with a guy whose mother still bought his socks—and was thrilled that someone else would be booking her son's haircuts in the future. Now, Rosie has moved on to a man who only needs her when his boss orders him to bring a partner to a corporate event. She always says: "When he gets his next promotion he'll be able to ease up and we'll see more of each other. At least he can take care of himself." Yes—and taking care of himself and his own needs (not yours) is exactly what he's doing, along with all the other Mr. Wrongs.

HE MAKES YOU LAUGH, BUT THE JOKE'S ON YOU IF HE'S FOOLING AROUND WITH OTHER WOMEN

You probably know some of the Mr. Wrong types already. You've dated them, your friends have dated them, you've read about them in the glossy magazines. But read on to find out more.

THE LOSER LIST IS ENDLESS

Some losers are easier to spot than others, but here's a rough guide to some of the most common ones in circulation.

1 MR. MARRIED MAN

Even if he isn't wearing a ring you'll soon know from the way he keeps looking at his watch, won't take you out in daylight, never suggests you meet his friends, and can't see you at the weekend that there are three of you in the relationship.

2

MR. UNAVAILABLE

This hardest-to-work-out-what's-wrong type, Mr. Unavailable, is closely related to Mr. Married Man. He's perfect for you in every way, except when you want something from him—like a bit of reassurance, or comfort, or even just a little bit of him. Emotionally, you might just as well be on separate continents, but you'll persevere because, after all, it's your fault for wanting too much. Right? Wrong!

3

MR. BAD BOY

Think Joey in "Friends." He's such good fun to be around and fantastic in bed. How could you not find him irresistible? Until the morning after when the phone doesn't ring. And three weeks later, when he finally calls, you find someone else's bra stuffed down the side of his sofa. He fixes you with that gorgeous naughty boy grin and says he's sorry. It won't happen again—and the tooth fairy is real.

4 MR. SEX ADDICT

Mr. Sex Addict has the same fixation with satisfying one part of his anatomy but he won't always need to be unfaithful to prove it, unless you consider centerfolds competition. This man has never found a way of expressing what he's feeling except through sex: if he wants a cuddle he thinks he wants sex; if he's scared he thinks he wants sex; if he wants you to understand him—you've guessed it, sex again.

Of course if you're not around to have sex with he's perfectly capable of satisfying himself with the help of his internet or phone friends.

5 MR. UNRELIABLE

This loser doesn't really need you to be around much. Out of sight is out of mind as far as he's concerned. He may love being with you but don't kid yourself that you can count on him, because he is still a kid at heart. He'll break his promises because he had his fingers crossed and forget everything important you tell him—including to turn up.

MR. NEEDY

Mr. Needy will turn up and keep on turning up, even when you'd rather he didn't because you'd like the occasional moment to yourself. From the outside this sensitive, open guy may look like Mr. Right, especially if you've just escaped from one of these other unsavory types. But the steel in his eyes when he says he's so in love with you he'd die if you ever left him is likely to give you the shivers sooner or later. He'll satisfy your craving for sandwiches at 2 a.m. if you'll satisfy his need for round-the-clock approval.

In other words, once you're hooked, it's tough to escape from this man. He doesn't just want to be in your bed. He wants to be in your DNA and he wants you to get rid of everything else that might claim a nanosecond of your attention, whether it's work, friendships, social life, or hobbies.

LONELY HEARTS

Ask yourself this: If your friends were dating any of the following characters, or you came across their CVs in the lonely hearts ads, would any of them seem like a good catch? Unlikely!

High roller looking to share some adrenaline with girl who's happy whether she's holding my chips at the casino or my towel at the surf beach. I've more than enough excitement for the both of us and that's what will thrill you. **Contact: Mr. Action Man**

FEW PERSONAL ADS WILL BE AS HONEST AS THE EXAMPLES HERE, SO BE SURE YOU ALWAYS READ BETWEEN THE LINES WHEN SEARCHING FOR MR. RIGHT

My wife really doesn't understand me—but you and I know exactly what we need. Love, sex, and secrecy, and there's no need for either of us to stay for breakfast. **Contact: Mr. Married Man**

Lonely guy in the wood seeks playmate. Life will be a fairytale if you'll just join me in stopping the world so we can escape together. We'll live alone on nectar and 1001 stories of how I've been misunderstood, misused, and misled. **Contact: Mr. Needy**

Unattached, uninhibited, unbelievably gorgeous guy available for anything you like—apart from comfort, communication, commitment, and caring. **Contact: Mr. Unavailable**

IT'S IMPORTANT TO LEARN FROM PAST MISTAKES, WHICH MEANS BEING CAREFUL NOT TO FALL INTO THE TRAP OF SIMPLY SWINGING FROM ONE BREED OF LOSER TO ANOTHER

Trophy girlfriend required for confused Casanova. I'll woo you, win you over, and treat you to the time of your life. But no strings attached—the only place you'll ever tie me down is in bed. **Contact: Mr. Bad Boy**

Hooked on sex. Wanna hook up with me and share my passion for phone sex, chat-room sex, kinky sex, two-ways, three-ways, anyways, porn shops, and round-the-clock masturbation? If you'll be my centerfold, I'll let you watch me get off on everything but loving sex with you. **Contact: Mr. Sex Addict**

Will you adopt me? Disorganized male missing home seeks grown-up to take him, his career, finances, social life, and wardrobe in hand. Ideal partner for any girl who wants to practice having kids. **Contact: Mr. Unreliable**

Fearless male, looking for followers. I ought to be running the country, but I'll settle for running your life. I'll take charge in the bedroom and beyond. Just don't call me a control freak—or do anything I order you not to. **Contact: Mr. Controlling**

LOSER, LOSER, LOSER

The list of losers just goes on and on. And while the characters listed here are some of the most common Mr. Wrongs, you may well find the species between your sheets turns out to be a combination of several of them.

MR. ME

Mr. Me's only real love object is himself. Watch him walk past a mirror. He can't! At least not until he's cast a critical look at himself to make sure his profile is as gorgeous as it was when he admired it in the car mirror two minutes ago. You're there simply to make him look good, and he loves himself more than he'll ever, ever love you.

MR. CONTROLLING

This is a troublesome character to deal with because all us girls brought up on fairy-tales—from Cinderella through to *Pretty Woman*—like our Mr. Rights to be Strong. It may therefore take some time to realize that this guy's not only in the driving seat, he's got the map, the key to the CDs, and the money for the toll. And don't dare argue about the route or you'll see some true road rage.

MR. ACTION MAN

Mr. Action Man is madly in love with himself and his action-packed life, but the only action you're likely to see is secondhand. He wants you to fill his flask, not his thoughts, and he'll enjoy displaying you along with the silver trophies in his cabinet.

MR. OPINIONATED

This set-in-his-ways guy really ought to have lived two centuries ago when his overwhelming need to get people to see things his way might have been more appreciated—instead of having to drag his soapbox around with him. You're not his lover. You're simply an audience for his views.

REMEMBER: MR. RIGHT SHOULD CARE JUST AS MUCH ABOUT YOU AS HE DOES ABOUT HIMSELF

MR. MARRIED-TO-MY-JOB

As for Mr. Married-to-my-job, this workaholic lover may well be available around the clock at the office, but he is wholly unavailable to you—both physically and emotionally. And if you dare challenge the hours he spends in the arms of his real love (work), he'll insist you're jealous of his career or ungrateful for the sacrifices he makes to keep you in splendid style.

MORE BENIGN LOSERS

At the other end of the serious scale are the guys whose habits may be horrible but usually aren't harmful. Maybe he is a slob who never puts the toilet seat down after him but it's your long hair blocking the plughole and stopping the water from running away. Or he loves gadgets and wants to take everything apart? But you've got more used-and-discarded lipsticks than the nearest mall. It's crucial to know that perfection only ever happens in Hollywood—and only then because the moment Mr. and Ms. Right overcome all the odds to get together the credits start to roll. It's also important to remember that, as well as love, real-life relationships require humor, tolerance, and enough grown-up wisdom to recognize the difference between the guy who occasionally takes a little effort to get moving and the couch potato who'd rather spend every evening and weekend of his life with his Playstation friends than with you.

NOBODY IS PERFECT (THIS INCLUDES YOU) SO TRY TO RECOGNIZE THE DIFFERENCE BETWEEN ANNOYING FOIBLES AND FATAL FLAWS IN YOUR SEARCH FOR MR. RIGHT

SERIOUS LOSERS

There are other losers with addictions—alcoholics, gamblers, drug addicts, men addicted to violence—that you may have come across, but this book is not about them. If your man has a problem that means he's breaking the law, causing you psychological harm, or posing any kind of physical threat, then he needs professional help. The way he behaves is his responsibility, not yours. But if getting him out proves difficult, don't hesitate to seek out some help and support for yourself.

THE LOSER QUIZ

To help you focus on whether his behavior makes you feel sick to the stomach or just a little uptight, try the following "Are you into a loser?" quiz. That should quickly help you realize whether he's worth keeping.

WHAT'S HE LIKE WHEN YOU'RE AROUND YOUR FRIENDS?

1 We only see each other in dark parking lots so he's never seen, never mind met, my friends. ☐

2 He doesn't like me spending time with them when I could be with him so we don't see much of them now. ☐

3 He's nice to their faces, but then criticizes them behind their backs. ☐

4 He flirts shamelessly and I get quite embarrassed. ☐

5 He likes and respects them and we often go out and have a great time with them. ☐

YOU'VE JUST MADE LOVE. WHAT DOES HE DO NEXT?

1 He reaches for the Wet Wipes to clean himself, then asks me to check his jacket for hair. ☐

2 He tells me he can't live without me and falls asleep in my arms like a contented little boy. ☐

3 He wants us to watch the porn channel or look at sex mags until he's aroused enough for us to have sex again (and again). ☐

4 He locks himself in the bathroom so he can check his phone for texts without me seeing. ☐

5 Sometimes we talk, sometimes we fall asleep, sometimes we make love all over again. ☐

HOW'S HIS RELATIONSHIP WITH HIS EX-ES?

1 He talks about them constantly and seems really bitter.

2 He's still got all their numbers on speed-dial and likes to boast about how gorgeous they are.

3 He says he can't remember their names, in fact he sometimes forgets mine.

4 They're still very much in his life, keeping an eye on him. It's like dating a guy with seven big sisters.

5 He's in touch with a few and we've talked about why they were wrong for each other.

YOU GO ON VACATION TOGETHER. HOW DO YOU SPEND YOUR TIME?

1 Applying 60 SPF sunblock. His wife thinks he's at a conference in Stockholm.

2 Actually we don't. I go out alone while he catches up on his sleep, but once we're with the night crowd and he's had a few drinks, we have a fantastic time.

3 It's all a bit intense. He doesn't want to talk to anyone but me and there's no point going to the beach because he gets miserable if other guys look at me in my bikini.

4 I spend my time watching him watching other women.

5 We do a bit of everything and often consider calling work to say the airline has gone on strike and we can't get home.

SO HOW DOES HE MEASURE UP?

It isn't rocket science: every answer from 1 to 4 is a wake-up call that all is not well. It doesn't matter which boxes you've checked—unless they're all number fives in which case you can stop reading now and give this book to one of your needy friends. More than one or two checks in the 1–4 boxes and sooner or later your fairytale is likely to turn into a horror story.

HOW DOES HE MAKE YOU FEEL?

Next, let's take a look at the checklist below to identify and start to accept how your guy really makes you feel about yourself.

IF HE MAKES YOU FEEL BAD ABOUT YOURSELF, HE'S PROBABLY NOT THE MAN FOR YOU. YOU DESERVE TO BE MADE FEEL SPECIAL EVERY DAY

Here's the thing. No matter how hard you work at fooling yourself into believing he's right for you, and that with just a little more effort or hard work on your part you can make it right, you'll never really be able to fool your feelings.

We're all equipped with highly sensitive sonar systems which pick up vibrations from every relationship we have, everything that's said and done—both good and bad. So when we see our friends or family members pairing up with the wrong partners, our sonars start broadcasting distress signals on their behalf. And when we read articles about the tortuous ins and outs of the famous in love, we agree sagely that their relationships are likely to be over before the ink is dry.

So why don't we use this sonar system for ourselves? Well, mainly because we either don't want—or don't dare—to sit still long enough to hear and trust what our own feelings are telling us. After all, once we hear them, there's no excuse not to act.

FOR INSTANCE:

- Are you scared to argue with him because he says you're being disloyal?

- Does he make you feel you're being neurotic because you want to know where he was at 3 a.m. last night when your friends say they saw him out clubbing?

- Do you feel guilty for wanting to continue with your girls' night out each month because you know he'll be sitting home alone and miserable?

- Do you resent the vast amount of time he spends with his friends, colleagues, and family because he tells you nothing about them and has never even let you meet them?

- Do you feel isolated from other people and the things you've always loved to do?

- Are there lots of days when you feel really rotten about yourself because he finds fault with the way you look, speak, think, and/or behave?

- Do you feel empty and abandoned just after you've made love?

These are only a few of the warning signs that he's probably not the right one for you. This is not to say he won't be right for someone else. One girl's loser may be another girl's Mr. Right, depending on what you both bring to the relationship—which is what we're going to look at in the next chapter.

KEEPING A NOTE OF WHEN YOUR GUY MAKES YOU FEEL BAD WILL HELP YOU WORK OUT WHETHER HE'S WORTH KEEPING

THE WAY AHEAD

For now, all you need to do is focus on the way your relationship makes you feel. Why not start making a note of it in the back of your diary? It doesn't have to be anything heavy. Just promise yourself that every time you have one of those "Oh?" moments you'll scribble a sentence about it: what were you doing, what was he doing, and what were you feeling?

And if you start to find those negative feelings you have around him are stacking up, then you need to take steps to get rid of him. But then again, you already know that because you've taken the first step—why else would this book have caught your eye?

CHAPTER 2

ALL ABOUT YOU

If you serially attract losers, then there must be something wrong with men, right? Well, yes and no. Since there is no such thing as a "loser" period (one girl's loser is another's Mr. Perfect), there must be a lot within you yourself dictating the type of guy you attract and stay with. As easy as it is to blame the guy when things go wrong, it really doesn't do any harm to look at yourself, too.

A BIT OF HISTORY

Life may be like a box of chocolates, but finding true love is more like the recipe for your favorite flavor of ice cream—hard to find!

LONG INTO ADULT LIFE THE RELATIONSHIP CHOICES WE MAKE ARE AFFECTED BY EVERYTHING THAT HAS GONE BEFORE—ALL THE THINGS WE'VE EXPERIENCED, SEEN, HEARD, AND FELT

Finding the recipe for a successful relationship sounds simple and it would be if you always looked for a tub of creamy mint ice to bring out the best in your rich chocolate chip. But you don't, perhaps because your parents brought you up to believe that anything other than vanilla was the work of the devil. Or perhaps you were wearing green the day your dog died and have hated anything about the color ever since.

The point is that every love choice we make is based on our past. We may think we're searching for someone to complement us but often what we're actually looking for is someone to complete us:

- To confirm what we think we know about relationships.
- To bring back familiar feelings and re-live good times.
- To replay the past with us and, this time, make it right.

IT'S WORTH TAKING A CLOSE LOOK AT OURSELVES BEFORE WE LAY THE BLAME FOR OUR LOSING PATTERNS ON ANYONE ELSE

HAPPY FAMILIES?

Right after Jane's parents split up she started college. All around her, her fellow students were having a great time: off the parental leash at last, making loads of friends, joining clubs, socializing, and playing the field.

YOU NEED TO UNDERSTAND AND LOVE YOURSELF BEFORE YOU'RE ABLE TO HAVE A HEALTHY RELATIONSHIP WITH SOMEONE ELSE

Jane, on the other hand, met Paul in the college registration line and they spent the next three years living the life of a married couple. At the age of 18, her subconscious had decided he would make a perfect substitute for her fractured family. They spent most weekends at his parents' home and while mom and Jane went clothes shopping, dad and Paul worked on the cars. They were a perfect family, which probably explains why she was always uncomfortable making love with Paul. He had signed up as her lover and she had turned him into her brother.

It took Jane five years from starting college to really leave home...by leaving Paul. And at least as many years again to recognize that the ups and downs of her own love life might have more than a little to do with all the baggage from home that she was carrying around with her.

Whatever you think about Jane "wasting" the best partying years of her life, your choices are likely to have been just as influenced by your early life. Ask yourself this: in all the time you've been dating, how much thought have you given to what really attracted you to your guy? I don't mean the line you feed your friends about loving his smile, strong arms, tight ass, sense of style, or bank account (surely not?).

Look deeper than this to what it really is about him—his character, his behavior, the way he treats you, and the way you feel around him—that reaches right back and pushes all the right memory buttons in you. You need to identify which particular bit of your software is being triggered by your man's hard drive and start to understand why.

So before we go any further, try the exercise overleaf concerning your past relationships to help you start pinpointing your patterns.

IF YOU'RE SERIOUS ABOUT GIVING UP ON LOSERS, YOU NEED TO GET A HANDLE ON YOUR OWN HIDDEN AGENDA

LOOKING AT YOUR RELATIONSHIP HISTORY

Get a blank piece of paper and in the left hand column write the names of all the guys you've ever dated for long enough to be able to recall their positive and negative qualities.

Then draw three more columns and label them "good points," "bad points," and "feelings."

For each guy, think of the things you liked most about him and write them down in the good column. For instance, he might have been kind, generous, intuitive, funny, good in bed, full of energy...and so on.

The next column is the important one for now. What were the qualities you disliked? Was he critical, erratic, opinionated, absent, overcautious, lazy? Keep in mind when you do this that it doesn't matter what other people thought of each guy. Your "opinionated" might be someone else's "outspoken and honest." You don't have to be objective. Just remember how each relationship was for you.

The final column is for you to note down how each guy made you feel about yourself. Sexy, secure, and smitten, or maybe small, stupid, and sad? The chances are that there will be memories of both good and bad feelings. Just put them all down for now to get a good overview.

Now take a look at the last two columns—the qualities you disliked about your ex-es and the way those same guys made you feel. Are there items that keep coming up or that are similar enough to start looking like a repeating pattern?

Do you see anything in your relationship history which looks like you were trying to put into action what you think you know about relationships, attempting to re-create familiar feelings, or replaying the past to put it right?

ARE YOU HOMESICK?

Whatever your situation growing up, all the adult relationships around you provided you with role models that will have affected your views on love.

IN THE SAME WAY YOU COPIED THE WAY YOUR ROLE MODELS SPOKE WHEN YOU WERE LITTLE, YOU ALSO LEARNED FROM THE WAY THEY BEHAVED TOWARD YOU AND TOWARD EACH OTHER

Maybe your mom brought home a series of "dads" from whom you learned men can't be relied on to stick around. Or maybe your folks stuck to each other like glue, hating each other and themselves for not having the guts to either leave or change things. The little girl watching them therefore got the message that anger, resentment, and powerlessness are always going to be part of the package.

Some people have parents like Shirley. One day she overheard her mom accusing her dad of having an affair, which explained why, when she was looking for a stick of gum, she'd found a packet of condoms in her dad's car. After that she always knew when her dad was playing around again—she just kept checking the car for condoms. But she never said anything in case he got angry and stopped loving her, too.

Shirley's almost 30 now and her men always let her down in the end. Usually she finds out they're either Mr. Married Man or simply Mr. Unreliable.

Of course, you may not be subconsciously looking for your dad, like Shirley. You could be trying to be him instead. When Azmina's dad walked out, her mom went to pieces, so Azmina took on the role of the adult in her house, from which she learned that emotions are dangerous things. As a result, she never takes risks with her heart, instead dating Mr. Needy after Mr. Needy: guaranteed to stick around as long as she can bear to go on supporting them.

And then there's Katie with her addiction to vacation romances. While she's somewhere exotic the guys she meets seem great, but in real life they look as flaky as her suntan. She's after passion, not permanence—just like her mom.

IT'S TIME TO FACE UP TO SOME HOME TRUTHS AND KICK SOME OLD HABITS IF YOU WANT TO HAVE MORE LUCK WITH MEN

LOOKING FOR CLUES

Not all of us have such obviously sad stories as Jane, Shirley, Azmina, or Katie (although you almost certainly know someone who does). That doesn't mean, however, that our pasts aren't holding us back in some way.

Perhaps you were a middle child who felt ignored and therefore doesn't expect men to pay any more attention to you now—especially as you know you're still that same little girl inside? Enter Mr. Unavailable to satisfy your Ms. Needy tendencies.

Or maybe your caregivers didn't know how to show their love for you. What happened when you fell over or something frightened you? Did they cuddle you or demand you stop being a baby? Try not to blame them if they did the latter; their parents almost certainly did the same to them. However, you may now find it hard to show any kind of weakness as a result, no matter how bad you're feeling. And being a parent to Mr. Needy could be your way of trying to put the past right without even realizing it—giving him the kind of parenting you wanted for yourself.

What about when you achieved something you felt really proud of? Did your family celebrate with you, or say you were being boastful and vain? If they put you down, your fragile young self-esteem may have taken a knock it's never recovered from.

IF YOU FELT UNDERVALUED AS A CHILD, YOU MAY NOW SEARCH OUT A MR. BAD BOY. IF ONLY YOU CAN TURN YOURSELF INTO SOMETHING BETTER, HE'LL STICK AROUND, WON'T HE?

MORE PROGRAMMING

Now let's look at the other dusty suitcases in your psychological attic. The ones labeled school, college, friendship, first love, and so on.

IF YOUR FIRST EXPERIENCE OF LOVE WAS MORE "DEVASTATING DISAPPOINTMENT" THAN "YOUNG DREAM," YOU'VE PROBABLY KEPT YOUR HEART LOCKED UP EVER SINCE TO PROTECT IT

If there were bullies in your neighborhood and the only way you could cope was by fading into the wallpaper, you may still prefer not to stand out from the crowd or stand up for yourself. Mr. Controlling may therefore seem like the "perfect" guy for you. Or, for that matter, Mr. Action Man, or any other guy who needs you as an appendage, not a partner.

Think, too, about how things were at school. Did people treat you differently because of the color of your skin, the way you spoke, the way you dressed, or the fact that you studied so hard? If so, you probably still can't quite believe that Mr. Bad Boy really picked you—and you won't be surprised if he leaves because it's what you feel you deserve.

What about when you got your first job? Were you treated well and encouraged to succeed, or was your manager

HOW OTHER PEOPLE MAKE US FEEL HAS A HUGE IMPACT ON HOW WE VIEW OURSELVES

jealous and overbearing, constantly waiting for you to make a mistake in order to humiliate you in public?

And how was your first love? Did it all seem perfect, then he suddenly dumped you? And have you been avoiding laying yourself on the line ever since? It doesn't matter what makes him unavailable—his padlocked emotions, his addiction to sex, or the ring on his finger—as long as you can't ever have him, you know deep down you're safe.

ALL CHANGE

Starting to operate with your eyes wide open, and with your self-awareness fully charged, is a giant step toward building your self-esteem and taking control of your life—and that's where you're now capable of heading.

THE FASTER THE CARNIVAL RIDE, THE TIGHTER WE HANG ON TO THE RAILS. BUT CHANGE REQUIRES THE COURAGE TO LET GO

Now you've had an opportunity to think a little about your personal programming, take another look back at the relationship history exercise (see pp. 36–37). Think in particular about the feelings you noted in the last column: are there other times in your life when you've felt that way, too? And if so, what was it that triggered them?

You'd think we'd run as fast as we can away from the things that make us feel bad. But sometimes it's familiar feelings that we're unconsciously searching for. So why is this?

It's pretty simple: human beings are not that great at change. We prefer to know where we are and find routine reassuring.

WE HAVE IT IN US TO BECOME THE PEOPLE WE'VE ALWAYS WANTED TO BE, LIVING THE LIVES WE DESERVE TO LIVE, SO WHAT'S STOPPING US?

Things that are familiar help us to feel secure.

We all have the ability to change and adapt, to learn from the past, and to move on. That, after all, is what this book is about.

But we need plenty of encouragement and practical help. So much around us is changing every day that it's no surprise we sometimes feel too exhausted to tackle change in our own lives. When was the last time you changed your hairstyle, for example? And do you always make a beeline for the black colors when you're choosing pants?

Seeking the familiar is our way of feeling like we've still got some control when it's obvious that so much of what happens in our lives is way outside our control. There's no doubt that letting go requires a huge amount of courage, but you can't change until you do.

SELF-ESTEEM CHECK

At the heart of any healthy relationship is healthy self-esteem, and all of the things you've identified from your past will have had a huge effect on how much of this you have.

IF YOU DON'T ACCEPT AND LIKE YOURSELF, DEEP DOWN YOU WON'T EXPECT OTHERS TO LIKE OR ACCEPT YOU EITHER

Go through the checklist (right) to see how full your self-esteem bottle is. Are you still full of fizz, or did you go flat a long time ago?

If your self-belief is running on empty you may well feel that everyone else is prettier, sexier, or more clever than you; and that everyone else's relationships are easier and better than yours; and that you're getting just what you deserve from life.

There are plenty of days when you'd rather slouch about in your PJs than spend hours putting on your face, but you don't do it because you think that if he sees the bad-hair, bad-skin, bad-mood-you he'll be out of the door faster than you can say Bridget Jones.

Strangely, life often has a way of meeting our own expectations. So if your self-esteem is low and you can't see why any guy would want to spend time with you, they probably won't want to.

WHO LOVES YA BABY?

For each question, answer with "regularly," "sometimes," or "never."

If something goes wrong, do you assume it's your fault?

Are you waiting for people to find out that you're terrible at your job?

Do you watch your weight constantly and know life would be better if you were a few pounds lighter?

Do you struggle to believe any compliment is sincere?

Do you find it hard to say no to people?

Is it even harder to ask them to do something for you?

When little things go wrong, is your reaction totally out of proportion?

Do you feel as if you have no control over your life?

Do you feel you have to try hard to get people to like you?

Do you bend over backward to avoid arguments?

Do you find it hard to express your feelings?

Do you think happiness is something you have to earn rather than something you deserve?

IF YOUR SELF-ESTEEM IS LOW YOU'LL PROBABLY FEEL GUILTY ABOUT GIVING YOURSELF LITTLE TREATS

HOW DID YOU SCORE?

All of us have insecurities. That's normal. But we need to keep our sense of balance.

Mostly "regularly" and your self-esteem bottle is definitely more than half empty. You need to think about how you can turn "regularly" into "sometimes." See the next chapter for ideas.

Mostly "sometimes" and you're getting there. But look at the areas where you seem to be unsure of yourself and think of ways to start to turn your "sometimes" into "rarely."

Mostly "never." Hmm. This could be a good thing but are you 100% sure it's not you that's Unavailable, Unreliable, Controlling, or any other of the types we've mentioned?

GREAT EXPECTATIONS

It's a plain fact that no single relationship can provide you with everything you want, need, and dream of. So be careful not to expect too much in your search for Mr. Right. After all, he's gonna be Mr. Right, not Mr. Perfect. And certainly don't give up or let down your friends in pursuit of him.

Expectations are the other thing in your dusty attic that you need to sort out. You might have picked them up at the same time as all the other stuff we've been talking about. Or they could be more recent acquisitions—from films you've watched, books you've read, or all the deliciously conspiratorial conversations you've had with girlfriends about your love lives. Wherever they're from, it's best to send them straight to the dump, as they're definitely holding you back.

TEN MISTAKES WE ALL MAKE TOO OFTEN

1	Mix up excitement with love.	That quiver in your stomach isn't love. It's adrenaline. It's important to enjoy the catch as well as the chase.
2	Equate love to an orchestra crescendo.	Love may be more like a tune you've heard a hundred times and suddenly realize you adore.
3	Think there's only one perfect match.	Are all your friends the same people you played with when you were three? Life moves on, and so should you.
4	Confuse good sex with a strong bond.	Sometimes they go together and sometimes not. When you see him out of bed, do you still have something to say?
5	Put your guy on a pedestal.	He's got as many faults and foibles as you if you'd only take off those rose-tinted specs.
6	Buy into the Beatles: All you need is love.	You also need loyal friends and family, fulfilling work, an income, a home, and to be understood and appreciated.
7	Worry each time you fight that it's over.	There's nothing wrong with disagreeing, as long as you respect each other's views.
8	Judge the relationship on your last date.	So all the other things you've shared count for nothing? Surely your relationship is worth more than that.
9	Believe the right guy will change your life.	Remember that the rescuer of a drowning person is often dragged under, too. You need a partner, not a prop.
10	Think Mr. Wrong is better than no one.	No he's not. He's making you unhappy and is stopping you from finding Mr. Right.

If you don't believe the negative effects some of our favorite books and films can have on our levels of expectations, consider just how many of them feature women falling head over heels for losers. The biggest losers are those who die before they even get a chance to have a real-life relationship, like the lovers in *Out of Africa* and *Titanic*.

As for the singing nun in *The Sound of Music*: what are we supposed to make of her love life? She falls for Mr.—sorry, Baron—Almost Married-Man, Controlling, and Unavailable all in one. This guy is a snob, is horrible to his children, listens to no one, and has a bad temper.

And yet, just like Cinderella, our nun gets her man in the end—and we are so swept up in her gratitude, in their dramatic escape from the Nazis, and in the gorgeous music and scenery, that against all the evidence we believe they'll live happily ever after. The movies have an awful lot to answer for.

Don't worry though, it's good news that life isn't like the movies. Unlike our celluloid heroes and heroines we've usually got years—not hours—to get it right. So we should use the time wisely—to gain a deep enough understanding of ourselves to recognize when we're switched to automatic pilot:

JUST BEFORE WE MOVE ON, LOOK BACK AT YOUR LIST OF LOSING LOVERS AND RUN THE "TEN MISTAKES" TEST (P. 49) ON THEM. HOW MANY TIMES HAVE YOU BEEN WITH MR. WRONG FOR THE WRONG REASONS?

acting from our unconscious rather than our conscious feelings. It's good to go with your heart at times but all heart and no head is a dangerous combo when it comes to losing your loser and finding Mr. Right. The more your self-awareness increases, the less susceptible you'll be to all the influences we've looked at in this chapter.

CHAPTER 3

TAKING CHARGE

Time to take control then. And that means control of your own life, not his, because he is the only one who can do anything to change himself.

No matter how much time, trouble, and tears you're willing to put into making him over, it's pain down the drain unless he's dissatisfied being Needy, Unreliable, Bad—or Sad. In other words, he has to want to read this book, too, and understand what's pulling his strings in order to change.

SO WHAT'S KEEPING YOU?

As we learned in the last chapter, the more you understand yourself, the more able you'll be to take charge and move on. But perhaps you're stuck at the knowing-what-you-should-do-but-not-wanting-to stage. A bit like staring a plate of spinach in the face: your head and your heart are at war. This chapter is about changing your mindset to bring heart and head in line.

Debbie's been with Mike for almost 15 years and for 14 of them she's been telling everyone who'll listen she has to leave. Not that she hasn't tried to get away. She even went so far as to get married to someone else (not a recommended exit strategy). On her wedding morning Mike sent a vast bouquet with a note swearing she was the only woman for him and he'd love her forever. Even if Debbie's marriage hadn't been conceived in desperation, it was always going to struggle after that.

Sure enough, Debbie's Mr. Substitute quickly got the boot and she went back to

Mike. During their truly dismal decade and a half together Debbie even forgave him for leaving her when her dad was dying. He'd gone with his ex-wife to stay with friends, and five days passed before he even called. Apparently there were no phones in the city that he and his ex were visiting.

She's learned to live with the long list of women's names in his email address book and all the times the phone rings and the caller hangs up without speaking. She tolerates this Mr. Controlling's need to be involved in every nook and cranny of her life—and no longer complains (to him) about the fact that in 15 years she has only been to his place a handful of times and never met any of his friends, colleagues, or his adult children.

WITH ALL THE SCHEMING AND DREAMING IN THE WORLD, IT'S UNLIKELY YOU'LL EVER CHANGE MR. WRONG INTO MR. RIGHT

In the face of every single slight, every niggling doubt about her man's authenticity, Debbie reminds herself that Mike is funny, charming, sexy, and original—and clings to her myth that she might one day change him.

WHAT'S YOUR EXCUSE?

So, did Debbie's story (see pp. 54–55) touch a few raw nerves with you? For every day when we feel desperate or determined enough to announce we're leaving our loser, there are others when we are able to convince ourselves it's all going to be OK.

Part of the problem is that in order to keep the relationship going we've become expert at deceiving him, and ourselves, about how we really feel. Making excuses for not leaving is just an extension of that.

But in reality, if your relationship is making you feel anything other than happy and fulfilled, then it is broken and needs fixing big time. Losers stay losers because we let them. Think about how you felt when you started to fall for him—optimistic, happy, and carefree—and think about how you feel now—low, controlled, underconfident, and plain miserable. It's painful to recognize that eventually you will have to admit that it's not working out, and try to live life on your terms, not his.

THE ONLY PERSON WHO CAN DO SOMETHING ABOUT YOUR RELATIONSHIP IS YOU

THINK ABOUT WHAT YOU REALLY WANT

Take a look at the list on the next couple of pages and see if you're being held back by any of these traps. Almost all of them say more about you than the guy you're with. Ask yourself whether any of the traps you're in fit with what you now know about your own motivations.

YOU BELIEVE A LOUSY RELATIONSHIP IS BETTER THAN NO RELATIONSHIP

So you're scared of being alone? But aren't you even more lonely with your loser?

YOU'RE SCARED OF WHAT YOUR MR. NEEDY WILL DO IF YOU LEAVE

Eventually you will leave, even if, like Debbie, it takes you decades to decide to do it. You can't take responsibility for how he reacts, but you can and should take responsibility for being honest in your dealings with him.

YOU'RE ON A RESCUE MISSION

There are plenty of more deserving outlets for your charity than Mr. Unreliable. Where's his self-respect? Would you want to be someone's charity case?

YOU'RE SCARED OF INTIMACY AND MR. UNAVAILABLE DOESN'T CHALLENGE THAT

It is scary to get close to someone and let them get close to you, but the worst that can happen if you let love into your life is you get let down. The worst that can happen if you don't is that you never even know what it is to love and be loved in the first place.

HE'S A TROPHY BOYFRIEND WHO MAKES YOU LOOK GOOD

So he's a Bad Boy who behaves like a pig, but at least he's a rich pig with an impressive car. Would you give him the time of day if he was a penniless pig? Why not put your energy into getting rich enough to buy your own car?

YOU'RE IN THE COMFORT ZONE

Do you stay with him because it's great to have someone other than yourself to blame for everything that goes wrong with your life? Of course it saves you from taking responsibility for your own happiness. Ouch!

HE'S YOUR WAY OF REBELLING

Using him to prove a point demeans both him and you. Prove your point by being happy. It's so much more satisfying.

YOU OWE IT TO BOTH OF YOU TO BE HONEST ABOUT WHY YOU'RE IN THIS RELATIONSHIP

YOU LIKE THE ATTENTION OF YOUR FRIENDS ON YOUR "PROBLEM"

Do you really think so little of yourself that you need a problem to make you interesting to your friends—just like when you were a kid and enjoyed getting attention because you were sick.

YOU FEEL LOCKED IN

All those years together to untangle: as well as saliva, you share furniture, saucepans, photo albums, friends, and so many memories. It's too huge to even contemplate.

ADMITTING YOUR FEARS

We'll look at how to actually end a relationship in the next chapter. All you need to do for now is breathe deeply and take comfort by thinking of all the people you know who have managed to move on from a bad scene—some of them after half a lifetime.

POSTPONING THE INEVITABLE DOESN'T MAKE IT ANY LESS PAINFUL. IT MAKES IT FAR, FAR, WORSE. YOU OWE IT TO EVERYONE, AND MOST OF ALL TO YOURSELF, TO BE HONEST

Letting go of your losing habit can be very scary, especially from where you're standing right now. But isn't the alternative of staying with Mr. Wrong even scarier?

For instance, when Glenda got married for the second time, tears rolled down her cheeks as she said her vows. She and Jimmy had both left partners and been through hell and high water to get to this point.

Except Glenda wasn't crying for happiness. Five years later, when she left Jimmy, she admitted she'd been crying because she already knew she was doing the wrong thing. Jimmy had been her quick fix, bringing all the excitement of illicit love into her life, as well as a convenient escape route from the unhappy marriage she was already in.

She'd muddled love and lust—but knowing how much they'd risked to be together, how much pain they'd put themselves and others through, she didn't dare say "I don't." This actually meant more pain, bitterness, and money in the form of a second divorce.

THE MILLION-DOLLAR MAN

Look back now to the exercise you did on past relationships (see pp. 36–37) and make a note alongside each ex's name of when, in the course of that relationship, you knew he was wrong for you. Then make a note of how long it took to get past the making-your-mind-up dithering to actually Doing the Deed.

BELIEVE IT OR NOT, IT IS NOT ORDAINED THAT WOMEN SHOULD ALWAYS END UP WITH LOSERS, SO DON'T LOSE HOPE

Add up those months (or years, if you've had it bad). How much time and energy have you spent wanting out when you could have been doing something more fulfilling with your life? Enough to have written that book you always wanted to? Designed and built your house? Learned to speak another language? Been in a loving relationship with a man who makes you feel like a million dollars?

Hopefully you've come across couples whose example inspires you, if not among your own networks then in public life. And don't just look at their example, follow it! You already know what it is you're looking for in a relationship: just look back to the column of your relationship history (see pp. 36–37) where you jotted down the things you liked most about each of

THERE'S NO SUCH THING AS THE PERFECT MAN BUT THERE IS SUCH A THING AS THE PERFECT MAN FOR YOU

your ex-es. Are there qualities that crop up regularly? Are there things that you regard as essential?

If so, you have the start of your blueprint for a winning relationship, so no more making excuses to yourself.

COMMON DENOMINATORS

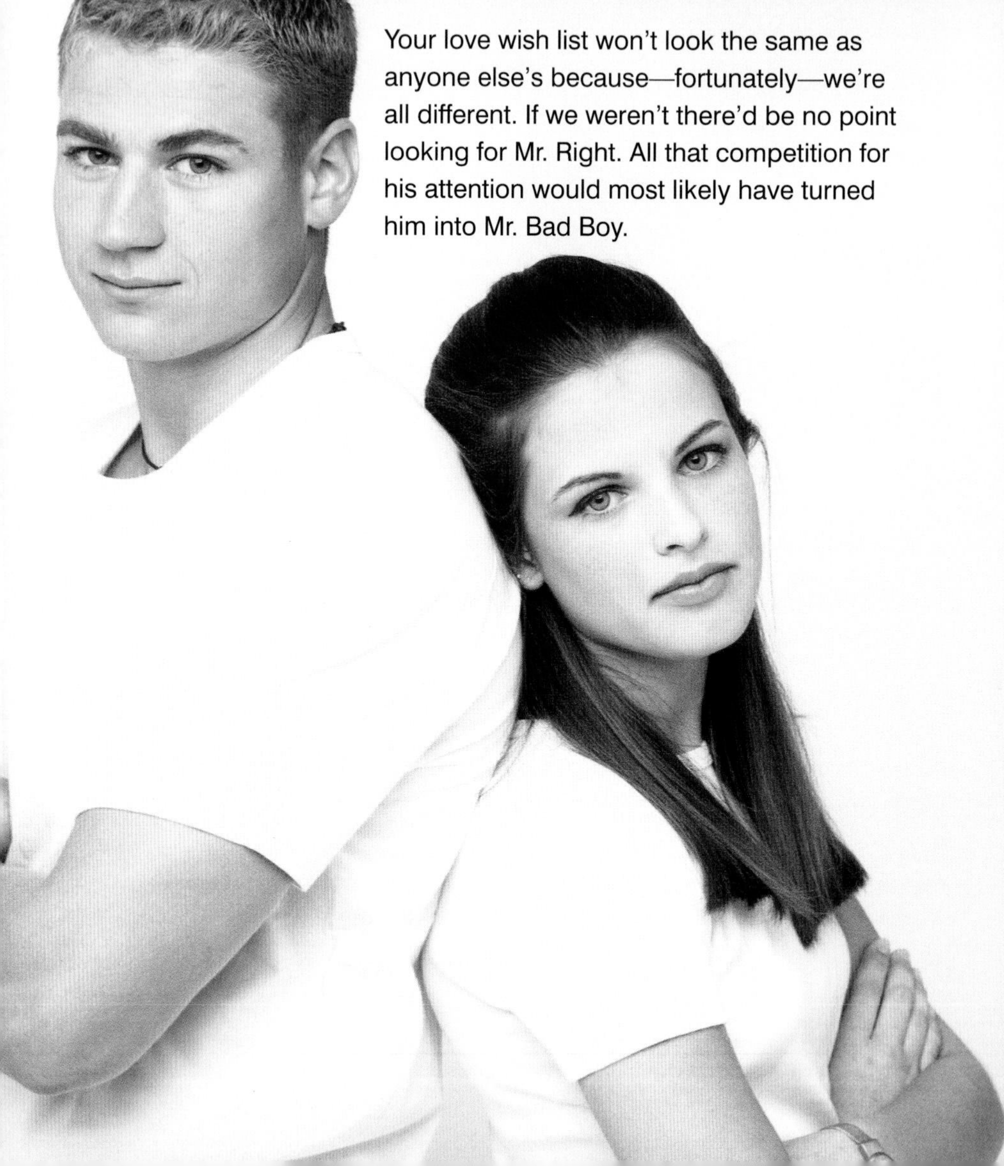

Your love wish list won't look the same as anyone else's because—fortunately—we're all different. If we weren't there'd be no point looking for Mr. Right. All that competition for his attention would most likely have turned him into Mr. Bad Boy.

But there are some common denominators—the building blocks of any healthy relationship—which are worth keeping at the forefront of your mind.

SUSTAINING: You value each other and care deeply about each other's well-being and happiness, so are prepared to work to make each other happy.

HONEST: You're able to be yourselves with each other and to show your vulnerabilities as you know they won't be taken advantage of.

ENHANCING: You know you are individuals but the love and trust you share brings out the best in each other so that you like yourselves even more in the relationship than apart. At the same time you both give each other space and permission to grow.

EQUAL: You may be very different people and bring different things to the relationship, but there is absolute equality of trust, of caring, of sharing, of respect, and of loving.

It sounds obvious but it's worth asking yourself whether you actually like your partner. Not love or lust after, but like. Enough for him to be a friend if he weren't your lover? If the answer's not an unequivocal yes, if you'd never choose a friend like him or you'd hate to have a child who was like him, you're with the wrong guy.

ALWAYS AND FOREVER?

Just a word about the absence of "always and forever" from the list of essentials. Allowing each other to remain individuals means taking a chance that you might grow in different directions. Sometimes if you can't negotiate changes, you have to just let each other go. Don't let fear that it won't be till death do us part stop you from taking a chance on Mr. Right, right here, right now.

BANKING ON LOVE

How does the man you're with measure up? Does he have the qualities you like in a man (see the "good points" list from pp. 36–37)? Or have you had to compromise on what you want from a relationship? Can you be yourself when you're with him?

If your heart still needs a bit of convincing as to whether or not he's the man for you, try the following "audit" to decide for sure if he's worth his weight in gold or simply draining you dry. Would life be richer without him in it?

CHECK HIS EMOTIONAL BANK BALANCE

For this exercise you need to draw up a blank copy of the chart below and keep it by your bed. Each night, before the lights go out, decide what your guy has paid in and taken out that day. For each item you list, give it a credit or debit score from $1–$10, depending on how the item made you feel. Credit is good and debit is bad with a capital B (for bankruptcy).

Keep the balance going for a week and then add up his totals. If he's overdrawn (like the guy below), or even hovering close to it, then close his account now.

REMEMBER: PARTNERS NEED TO "INVEST" EQUALLY IN A RELATIONSHIP TO KEEP IT EMOTIONALLY VIABLE

WORTH HIS WEIGHT IN GOLD?

It's handy to keep a written record of how much your man is investing in your relationship.

Date	Item	Credit	Debit
Monday	Noticed my new hairstyle	$2	
	Didn't say he liked it		$5
Tuesday	Called off our date as working late		$7
	Turned up after midnight, drunk, wanting sex, threw up, then fell asleep		$9
Wednesday	Scrubbed carpet where he threw up last night	$3	
	Sent flowers and groveling apology	$4	
	Too hung over to meet me (I didn't want to anyway!)		$2
Thursday	Kept me awake half the night moaning about his boss when knew I wanted to be fresh for a job interview		$4
	Woke me at 4 a.m. saying sex would help him sleep!		$6
Friday	Remembered to text to ask how interview went	$4	
	Bumped into him with his coworker. All he said was "What are you doing here?"		$10
	Big fight over phone—apparently I'm possessive		$10
	Totals	$13	$53
			$40 OD

BETTER OFF?

Old habits die hard—and along with them the get-up-and-go to get up and go. So if you're still having doubts about whether to get rid of your man, think seriously about what effect the relationship is having on you. Do you like yourself when you are with him?

Have you had to change what you eat, wear, or do to suit what he wants you to be? Are you able to see the people you want to when you want to? Can you express your views without fear? Do you have to make excuses for him to your family and friends? How often do you make allowances for him or readjust the boundaries of what you'll accept from him? More than feels OK?

Do you spend frustrating hours fretting, talking, or thinking about him? Deep down do you see yourself as his partner and lover—or more as his mother, maid, therapist, fan club, fall guy, punching bag, energy source, accessory, or sex kitten?

Remember that instead of being stuck in a rut with someone who's never really there for you, who confirms what losers the men in your life are, or who allows you to stay stuck in the past out of fear, you could be with a guy whose love would help you to be honest, happy, and the best you can be. That's a pretty powerful thought. So what's stopping you?

ONE OF THE GREATEST AFFIRMATIONS IS TO BE LOVED, VALUED, AND RESPECTED FOR WHO YOU ARE—NOT FOR WHO YOUR MAN WANTS YOU TO BE

CHAPTER 4

MAKING A CLEAN BREAK

When it comes to leaving a loser, the fire service has the right idea. Don't just blunder through the smog hoping good fortune will deliver you to the exit. Think ahead and plan your escape route down to the last detail.

Knowing your exit strategy is like taking out insurance against the tricks that many men play to get you to stay. If you stick to the small print they're less likely to be able to manipulate you into changing your mind at the last minute.

BREAKING UP IS NEVER EASY

HE MAY BE A LOSER BUT HE'LL TRY TO PERSUADE YOU TO SEE IT HIS WAY

Ending a relationship is always hard to do. But when breaking up with a classified loser, you're likely to face all sorts of extra hurdles. Knowing this and preparing for it in advance can help you clear the most likely hurdles (see right).

FOR INSTANCE:

- Mr. Controlling simply isn't used to anyone but himself calling the shots. He'll therefore do everything he can to talk you back where he thinks you belong: under his thumb.

- Saying the words "we're through" is likely to turn Mr. Unavailable into Mr. All Yours in one fell swoop. He'll suddenly focus 100 percent on how much you must be hurting—until the very next time you need him, that is.

- Mr. Bad Boy may give you his easy-come, easy-go shrug, but you can bet this isn't the last time you'll hear from him. He really needs to know that he's not losing his touch, so expect regular "casual calls" suggesting you get together for old time's sake.

NO MATTER HOW UNHAPPY YOU ARE IN YOUR RELATIONSHIP, IT WILL TAKE A LOT OF COURAGE TO TAKE THE BULL BY THE HORNS AND END IT. AFTER ALL, YOU'VE INVESTED A LOT OF TIME, ENERGY, AND LOVE IN HIM

- Since Mr. Sex Addict expresses his feelings through sex, he'll want to show you how much he's hurting the only way he knows how.

- Mr. Unreliable usually wants his mom when things go wrong. Oh, hang on—he thinks that's you!

- Watch Mr. Needy melt in a puddle of despair when you call it a day. He wants you to feel so sorry for him that you'll forget to leave him in your dash for the mop and bucket.

- As for Mr. Married Man: How dare you? It's up to him to do the leaving, as he's been saying he'll do since the day you met.

LOCATION, LOCATION, LOCATION

Avoid acting on impulse in terms of where you split up with your partner or you could end up, like Sally, finishing with her Mr. Unavailable two days after they'd flown into a paradise island for their first ever vacation together. Having spent so much on their dream getaway, neither felt able to "get away" once they broke up. So for the next 12 days it was a case of sun, sand, sea, no sex, and lots of sulking.

The first rule is to choose neutral ground where you won't get trapped. If he's at your place when you break the news, he can dig in for a marathon discussion of why you shouldn't do it—unless of course you're a willing and able black belt, or are ready to walk out on yourself!

His place ought to be out of the question, too, especially if you've shared some good times there. Before you know it you could be sitting on his bed, remembering those good times and trying to make him feel better...and we all know what happens next.

A public place with private corners, like the park or a coffee shop, is your best bet. There's no shared history to distract you, enough people to prevent an embarrassing scene (hopefully), and plenty of obvious escape routes—keeping you firmly in control of what's happening.

If you choose a bar or restaurant, don't be tempted to bolster your courage—or give your shaking hands something to fiddle with—by ordering alcohol. There is no quicker way to blur the sharp edges of your resolve—as well as your vocabulary. And don't forget the effects that wine and spirits have on emotions, stoking and heightening them at the very moment when you will most need to keep a tight lid on them to stay in charge. Go for an orange juice or a coffee instead—much safer alternatives.

TRY NOT TO DWELL ON THE GOOD TIMES YOU'VE HAD WHEN BREAKING UP AS IT'S LIKELY TO WEAKEN YOUR CONVICTION

NO SUCH THING AS PERFECT TIMING

Planning your exit means you shouldn't suddenly find yourself blurting out how you can't stand another minute in his company in the middle of a girlfriend's wedding—ruining her day as well as his.

BEWARE OF THE DANGERS OF OVER-PLANNING YOUR EXIT TO THE POINT THAT YOU END UP NOT ENDING IT AT ALL

Nor should it mean wrecking your career prospects, like Petra. When her frustration with her Married Man lover (who also happened to be her supervisor) boiled over, she sent him a no-holds-barred email to say why they were through—copying in most of the senior management team by accidentally using the "reply to all" button.

But neither does planning mean endlessly finding reasons to put it off for another few weeks. For instance, if you find yourself deciding you'll

BREAKING UP WILL HURT NO MATTER WHEN YOU DELIVER THE BAD NEWS

wait to avoid finishing with your partner at a time when love is all the rest of the world can think about—like Valentine's Day—be suspicious of your own motives. Choosing to delay the bad news—however kind your motives seem to you—risks you losing the conviction that should be propelling you into your future.

ARTIFICIAL DEADLINES

As for the deed itself, it's a good idea to set a time limit if you think he's likely to try and talk you in circles. Arrange an unbreakable date with friends to go on to; have your best friend call to say your dog's sprouted pink wings and you're needed urgently; or tell him during a lunch break so you've not only got an excuse to call time, but you have the bonus of not having to return alone to an empty apartment. Basically, do whatever it takes to avoid one of those desperate scenes where you end up spending hours trying to justify yourself and convince him this is the best thing for both of you. Such "discussions" are unlikely to lead anywhere constructive.

PREPARING THE SCRIPT

It's a good idea to prepare how you are going to break the news to him—what exactly are you going to say? However much of a loser you think he is, he'll have his reasons for wanting to stay with you and for changing your mind.

TRY YOUR BEST NOT TO LET HIM LEVER UNCERTAINTY THROUGH THE CRACKS IN YOUR ARMOR

He's likely to react by trying to:
- Take apart your reasons for ending it.
- Convince you you've got it wrong.
- Insist you're as much to blame as him.
- Swear it'll be better if you give it one more chance.

If you're absolutely clear about what you want to say, you're less likely to get side-tracked into explanation, self-justification, remorse, or any of the other cul de sacs which could divert you from the straight and narrow.

The Do's and Don'ts list (see pp. 80–81) should help you to write the "script" or at least a draft of it.

LOOK HIM IN THE EYE?

Really consider whether you feel up to the challenge of telling your partner face to face, especially if this is not the first time you've tried to break up with this guy. Of course, meeting face to face is fairer, but if you're uncertain of your ability to follow through, to deal with his response—or one of the biggest problems with the relationship has been his ability to manipulate you—then give yourself permission to send him a letter or text message.

IF THE ONLY WAY YOU'RE EVER GOING TO BE ABLE TO BREAK UP IS AT A DISTANCE, GO FOR IT. IT'S BETTER THAN DOING NOTHING

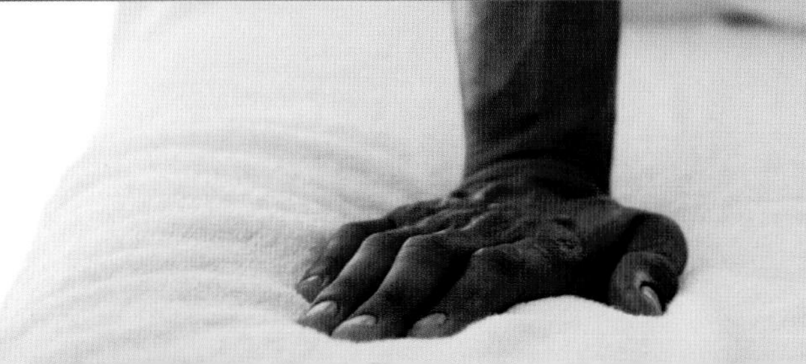

WRITING THE RIGHT SCRIPT

- DO keep the focus on yourself. If you stick to saying what you feel rather than what he's done (or not done), there's less chance of him challenging you. For instance, say "I feel frustrated that you're not able to be there for me a lot of the time" rather than "You're never there."

- DO be clear, honest, and firm. It's tempting to tell kind lies to try and make you both feel a bit better. But if you're not direct it's easier for him to argue you into knots.

- DO write the script down and practice it. This way, you don't get distracted by him trying to wrest control from you. If he tries to interrupt, insist clearly that he lets you finish.

- DON'T lay blame. You are both responsible for the relationship. You had reasons for choosing your loser, as he had for choosing you. Blame will get you nowhere but going around in circles.

- DON'T draw it out. A swift, clean extraction is always kinder in the long run than dithering.

- DON'T get into a dialog that's going nowhere. A discussion may undermine your resolve.

YOU KNOW WHAT YOU WANT SO DON'T DIGRESS FROM THAT OR FEEL YOU NEED TO OVER-JUSTIFY IT

DEALING WITH HIS REACTION

Your Mr. Wrong is unlikely to sit back and take your rejection of him without wanting some discussion. And this is where preparing your lines can help you stand your ground. You've told him how you feel, and you have an absolute right to those feelings. You also have the right to end a losing relationship.

So if he starts to argue with you, use the stuck record technique:

You: I told you, I'm ending this relationship.
Him: But you said you love me.
You: It's just no longer right for me so I am ending this relationship.
Him: So are you saying you've stopped loving me? I want to know why, what have I done?
You: This is about my feelings that this relationship is no longer right for me so I am ending it.

...and so on.

The minute you give him too much information, for instance by responding to his questions, you are giving him an opportunity to prolong or take control of the debate.

BODY TALK

If you meet him in person, it's important to check that your words are reinforced by your body language. No matter how many times you replay your record, he's got a hook to reel you in on if your eyes are darting desperately around the room or you're squirming in your chair like a fish on the end of a line.

It can be especially hard for girls to shift body language into neutral. From an early age we've learned to want to please, to smile, and to be generally accommodating. But this is one occasion when you can't afford to be. Control what your body's saying by acting out this checklist:

- Take a deep breath.
- Put your face in neutral.
- Sit up straight.
- Look him in the eye.

NO MATTER HOW MUCH HE TRIES TO TURN ON THE CHARM OR APPEAL TO YOUR SOFTER SIDE, REMAIN TRUE TO YOUR INITIAL INTENTION

STAY STRONG

It becomes even harder if your partner reacts strongly, especially if he gets upset. One of our deepest human instincts is to want to help and make things better when we see someone in distress. It's even true of total strangers, so it's all the harder when the person in pain is a man we know. Every fiber in your body might be urging you to comfort him but don't give in.

Instead, you need to put on a second record in your head and keep it playing. Its theme tune is: his reaction is not your responsibility.

It is not up to you to take his hurt, anger, disappointment, or confusion away.

If you do get a strong reaction that shocks, surprises, or scares you it may help to remind yourself that, like you, he's probably carrying a huge amount of baggage from previous relationships. You're possibly fielding the fallout from a whole lot of other issues in his life, as well as from your own relationship with him.

OTHER POSSIBLE REACTIONS

the "so what?" guy

There's another kind of reaction you need to be prepared for—and it's a favorite of many losers out there: the shrug that tells you he's not going to fight you, resist you, or give you anything back at all. You may even have used this technique yourself at some stage to convince a guy that "unattainable you" is the one he really, really wants.

Wanting what we can't have is human instinct (albeit a negative one), so now that the tables are turned, you're likely to feel rejected, whether his deadpan response is genuine or not.

It is crucial to hold your nerve here and not fall into the trap he may be setting for you—to make you want to try and win him back. You don't want him back, remember?

hidden potential

It's also worth a word about those rare occasions when your loser suddenly seems to have winning potential after all. You may well have picked up this book because you have a long track record of picking the wrong guy. But just occasionally, the shock of your "bad news" can be enough to stop a guy hard enough in his tracks to consider the direction his own life is taking. Like you, he has the capacity to change himself if he really wants to.

Do not confuse any such moment with what can be called the "sex=sympathy syndrome." Most of us have been guilty of this at some time: you've been dreading ditching him but he takes it so well that, warmed by the first real moments of connection in months, you end up back in bed. And have to do it all again the next day.

But if both your heart and your head tell you not only that he's capable of change, but also that reassessing your relationship together could bring real results for the future, then suggest you see a counselor together. The patterns we live by, however ingrained, all have the capacity to change with a little effort and know-how. If he's serious about you and willing to try and work things through, he'll agree. If not, there's no swifter way to flush out a faker.

DEALING WITH YOUR OWN REACTION

Be warned. It may have been you who's done the deed, but that doesn't mean you'll feel any less pain than him. Even your best friends—knowing how long you've wanted to shake him off—will probably be expecting to celebrate rather than commiserate with you and are likely to be surprised if they see you're hurting.

LOSS HAS ITS OWN PATTERNS AND TIMETABLE, AND THE ONLY SURE WAY TO COME OUT THE OTHER SIDE IS BY GOING THROUGH IT, AS PAINFUL AS THAT CAN BE

It's just a plain fact that the end of even the most awful relationship involves loss and therefore a mourning period. You haven't only lost your boyfriend, but also all the possibilities you once imagined for the two of you, as well as a whole lot of practical things like shared friends, plans, hobbies—and possibly even your home.

So don't try to deny or block out your feelings, however unexpected or unwelcome they are. And if your family or friends seem unsympathetic, show them this page and point out that you need their sympathy and support to get through this feeling of loss before you'll be ready to rebuild.

ALLOW YOURSELF PLENTY OF QUIET TIME AT HOME TO DEAL WITH YOUR GRIEF, AS WELL AS ORGANIZING LOTS OF FUN ACTIVITIES OUT AND ABOUT WITH YOUR FRIENDS TO HELP TAKE YOUR MIND OFF IT ALL

LOSS IS A ROLLER COASTER

Going through loss really is like jumping on the roller coaster at the carnival. One minute you'll be up in the clouds, the next down in the dumps. The only thing you can be sure of is that someone else is in the driving seat and you are wholly out of control.

WHEN YOU FEEL OVERWHELMED, LOOK BACK THROUGH THIS BOOK TO REMIND YOURSELF WHY YOU ENDED THE RELATIONSHIP

It's important to realize that there will be occasions after ending a relationship when your emotions may feel hugely out of proportion to your situation. In fact, you may feel completely overwhelmed. Unlike some emotions, loss seems to be cumulative. You're not only mourning the loss of your partner, but possibly everyone and everything else you've ever lost—from deceased relatives, to the dad you never knew, to the dog that ran away when you were a kid.

As your feelings hurtle up and down and you dread what's coming around the next corner, bear in mind that there is no such thing as a never-ending ride. Sooner or later—however impossible it seems right now—your carriage will come to a halt and you'll be able to climb off safely. The old cliché that time is a great healer rings true, so just try to remember that you will get through this.

KEEP TELLING YOURSELF THAT WHAT YOU'RE GOING THROUGH IS PERFECTLY NORMAL

The other important thing to remember about roller coasters is that you should never try to climb off them while they're moving! There is no short cut, and you will only end up hurting yourself more than the pain caused by staying on. So just strap yourself in as safely as you can for the ride. Every emotional journey will be different but some of the stages that almost everyone goes through are listed in the "Roller Coaster Stages" (see pp. 90–91).

ROLLER COASTER STAGES

shock and denial

Even though you knew it was coming, your first reaction may be disbelief. You may not want to talk about it or even think about it. Or you may be surprised to discover how upbeat you feel—as if you've suddenly got the energy to reorganize and redecorate your entire apartment. There's no need to feel guilty about feeling good. Shock is nature's way of helping us cope with pain: what you're experiencing is very much like when people throw themselves into practical details after the death of a loved one due to their inability to mourn at that precise time. Everything in its own time.

why me?

Here come the first of the tears as you descend into feeling sorry for yourself and wondering why bad things always happen to you and what it is about you that attracts so many losers. This is the time to just go with the flow and be kind to yourself. It's also the time to read back through the last two chapters to remind yourself exactly how (and why) you got to this point in the first place.

anger and blame

Feel the fury! Now you've stopped thinking it's your fault and are ready to believe it was all about him. Anger's a useful emotion so long as you find ways of expressing it without hurting him, you, or anyone else. Hurl as many objects (preferably soft!) as you like at the wall, pulverize those pillows, and scream obscenities at an imaginary version of him in the privacy of your own room. By all means, remember all the things he did to upset you, as long as you're able to recognize when the time comes to move on from being mad.

guilt and sadness

First it was his fault, now it feels like yours. Along with sadness, you start to feel guilty. You'll be doubting yourself, wondering what's wrong with you and whether there was something else you could have done to make the relationship work. These feelings make you especially vulnerable to wanting to get back in touch with him. Instead, you should stick with getting in touch with yourself.

Try to accept your situation, learn from it, implement change as a result of it if necessary, and move on.

the pit

Warning, warning! The tears you've already shed are nothing compared to what you're about to go through as you hit the bottom of your roller coaster. There may now be times when you feel terrified that your grief is so deep and that your emotions have spiraled seemingly out of control. This is the time to retreat to your comfort zone, whether that be the bed or your sofa. Lock all the doors. Play all "your" tunes. Weep over old photographs. Re-read his letters. But as you allow yourself to wallow in misery, don't forget to set the timer. You need to set boundaries around

FEELINGS OF GUILT CAN BE POSITIVE: BY ACKNOWLEDGING YOUR SHARE OF RESPONSIBILITY, YOU GIVE YOURSELF THE POTENTIAL TO LEARN AND MOVE ON

these periods in the pit so you don't get stuck there. Promise yourself you'll let yourself wail for two hours if needed but that you'll then meet your buddies for dinner, or run a deep bath, light the candles, and up the tempo on the CD player.

acceptance

Reaching this point doesn't mean you've stopped feeling sad, but the extremes of emotion are now behind you. As you rise up on the roller coaster, you get the bigger picture. Now that you know yourself better, you start to see more clearly why you and he didn't work, and you accept that you were definitely wrong for each other.

letting go

It may be months before you can find one of his hairs on your sofa without weeping. But life is starting to get better again and—more importantly—you not only believe you'll be OK, you know you are OK.

TIGHTEN YOUR SAFETY BELT

As you ride the roller coaster, the safety belt holding you in should be this: never ever act while you're feeling emotional. There will be many times when you yearn like you've never yearned before to pick up the phone, engineer a "chance meeting," pour out your heart in a long letter, or turn up on his doorstep and let him sweep you back into his arms. But don't.

When you have a tough life decision to make—whether about work, choosing somewhere to live, or taking out a loan—what do you do? You often sleep on it to make sure you are acting from your head as well as your heart. So why allow yourself to act on impulse at a time when your emotions are being pushed about all over the place?

THE POWER OF WORDS

There are several things you can do at those moments when you're tempted to jump off the roller coaster and back into his arms. One is to use word power. Whenever your feelings overwhelm you, get some paper and write your ex a letter. Write ten letters if you like. But then immediately seal them all and give them to your best friend or a parent with strict instructions they are not to be sent or handed back to you no matter how hard you plead until you are once again "of sound mind."

Alternatively, you could ask the same friend to sit and listen for an evening while you try to convince her why you should see him again—probably through tears. Then sleep on what you've said and see how much more clear-headed you feel about it the next day, now that so many of the emotions have been released. Things really can look different in the morning, including the calendar on the wall, which should be showing in red pen that you have just survived another day without him. Well done.

ANY MAJOR DECISION THAT YOU MAKE WHILE YOUR EMOTIONS ARE RUNNING HIGH IS LIKELY BE THE WRONG ONE, SO HOLD OFF FROM TAKING ANY DRASTIC ACTION

THE RIDE OF YOUR LIFE

The following survival tips should help you stay the course of your emotional roller coaster ride. Keep them at hand to reassure you in your moments of doubt.

REMEMBER TO KEEP BUSY

Not so busy that you stay in denial, but neither so quiet that you have time to wallow in all the things you feel you've lost along with your loser. You need activities as well as downtime.

PREPARE FOR IRRATIONALITY

You may think you're coping with losing him, your job, and your aunt in the same week but then you find yourself weeping just because you've broken your nail. Surprise, surprise: these emotional responses are not entirely unrelated.

TALK LESS?

Recognize when talking about him helps and when it's just reinforcing how bad you feel. The first is OK. The second is when you should dig in the garden, do some exercise, or go out somewhere with friends.

REDISCOVER YOURSELF

Make contact again—humbly—with all those things you ditched for him, whether friends, interests, or dreams. And make a note to self: when you do find Mr. Right, do not make the same mistake again.

REMEMBER HIS BAD POINTS

Write a list of all the bad things he ever did to you and stick it on the phone so you can't lift it without reminding yourself why you ditched him. It's a good idea to do this during your "anger and blame" stage as it could help you deal with the pent-up negative energy.

LOVE YOURSELF

Write positive, reinforcing messages to yourself to stick on the mirrors around your house, on the fridge, and by your bed. How about: "I don't have to settle for less," "I can cope without him because I did before," or "I'll never find Mr. Right if I stay with Mr. Wrong."

BE POSITIVE

Focus on all the good things that happen to you every day—that frothy cup of latte on a cold winter morning or the perfume of flowers on a summer's evening, making someone laugh, the comfort of your cat or dog snuggling up to you. And, above all, allow yourself to have fun.

USE THIS OPPORTUNITY TO CHANNEL YOUR PENT-UP ENERGY AND EMOTION INTO DOING THINGS YOU'VE BEEN MEANING TO DO FOR AGES, WHETHER THAT'S SPENDING MORE TIME WITH FRIENDS, GETTING FIT, OR TAKING UP A NEW HOBBY

A BEAUTIFUL FRIENDSHIP?

It's very possible that somewhere along the route the suggestion that you and he can stay friends will be made. But beware: there are usually only two reasons someone says "We can still be friends."

HOWEVER WONDERFUL YOUR FRIENDS, THERE MAY COME A TIME WHEN YOU FEEL YOU'VE LEANED ON THEM ENOUGH AND THAT IT WOULD BE BETTER TO TURN TO SOMEONE MORE OBJECTIVE

The first is you're feeling bad that he's feeling sad. And not only bad, but guilty. Agreeing to stay friends is your way of making yourself feel better. It won't help him get the clear message that you're through. In fact, it's more likely to confuse him. Plus it will put the brakes on his journey through the stages of loss, slowing up his recovery, so is really quite unfair.

The second relates to that traitorous corner of your heart that somehow escaped Chapter 3's discoveries and still clings to a glimmer of hope that he might change, you might change, or the whole world might change just enough to make it better. He won't, you won't, and it won't, so it's time to let go of that hope. Holding on to your fantasy will just keep your recovery on indefinite hold—your roller coaster car with the brakes on while high in the sky.

AN END—AND BEGINNING—IN SIGHT

Bear in mind that all roller coasters are different. Yours might only be a few ups and downs, it may involve half a dozen loop-the-loops, or you could find yourself tumbling back toward the pit—roller coasters do sometimes send you in reverse. What they can't do, however, is turn back time. Every switch in momentum you survive is one you will never have to go through again. And even when it feels like three steps forward and two back, remember that one step is still better than none, which means it's progress.

However, if you really do feel as though you might be getting stuck in a rut of depression, don't be afraid to seek professional help. Going to counseling is not an admission you can't cope, but rather a constructive way to help yourself move on.

Counselors are highly trained, are more distanced from your problem, and have the skills not just to listen and comfort you, but to help you find your own answers and learn to support yourself, without a loser in sight!

CHAPTER 5

THE SINGLE LIFE

There's never been a better time to be single. If you had been born 50 years ago you'd be as rare as a teenager without attitude. But with so many people now choosing to marry late, and half of those who tied the knot early now becoming free again, singles are not only common, but sought-after and well-catered for. So since you've got the T-shirt, you may as well grab a red pen and paint on the slogan: "Single and satisfied." And here's how...

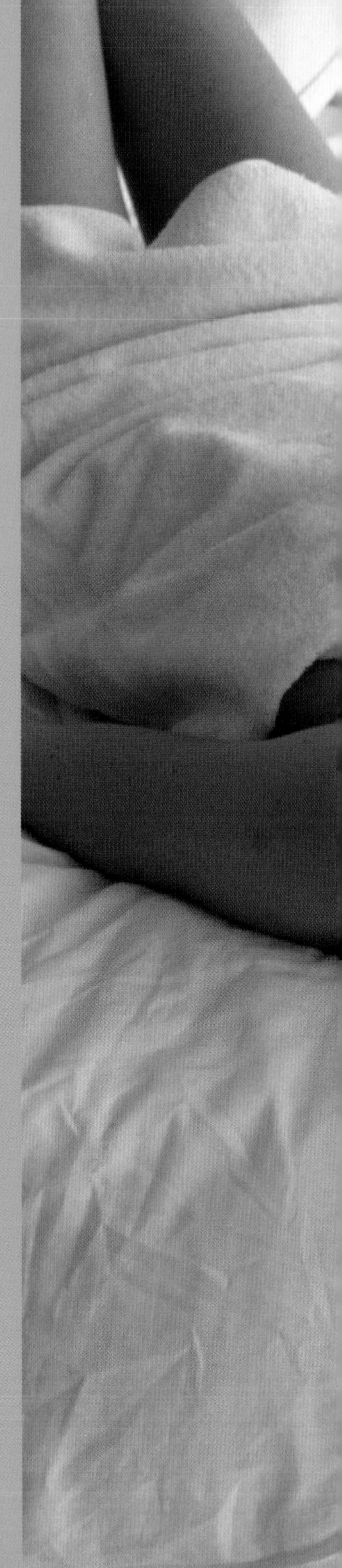

A TALE OF TWO SINGLES

Siobhan and Izzie are both newly single but they couldn't be more different. For Siobhan, every day without a man in her life is a wasted day. Every month that passes without her meeting Mr. Right takes her closer to some imaginary notion that she'll be stuck on the wrong side of the platform, forced to watch the Love Train leave forever without her on board. Every happy ending for someone else is a reminder that she's failed to find her own happy ever after—which can make her pretty miserable company most of the time.

POTENTIAL PARTNERS TEND TO TAKE US, OR LEAVE US, ACCORDING TO OUR OWN VALUATION OF OURSELVES

By contrast, Izzie gets invited everywhere by everyone. She might prefer to be in a relationship, but until she finds someone to do that with, she makes everyone laugh with outrageous stories about her search for Mr. Right—and all the Mr. Wrongs she has encountered en route. Unlike Siobhan, it doesn't seem to have occurred to her to put her life on hold while she waits for a guy to come along.

These examples are living proof of the way other people judge us according to how we judge ourselves. While Siobhan's desperation is as effective as a

12-foot fence at keeping people away, Izzie's determination to get on with life is like a welcome mat. Her energy, humor, and zest for life make her hugely attractive to the people she meets, including plenty of potential boyfriends. Moral of the story: Act as if you're happy, successful, and satisfied and not only will the world believe that you are, and treat you that way, but in time you'll discover that it's not a confidence trick at all—you really are all of those things.

Siobhan and Izzie's attitudes to themselves have a lot to do with their self-esteem—a part of us that can take a battering while we're in an unhealthy relationship and, again, as we emerge from one—perhaps feeling foolish, hopeless, or unlovable.

BE GOOD TO YOURSELF

"Esteeming" yourself means first giving yourself all the things that you'll want to give to your Mr. Right when he comes along—love, trust, value, and respect. So if you feel you don't lavish enough of these things on yourself, make a start by trying the self-esteem boosters on the following spread.

BRILLIANT BOOSTERS

The world sees singles as synonymous with fun and excitement—the opposite of cozy and conservative coupledom, so enjoy it!

ALL THAT ENERGY YOU WERE PUTTING INTO KEEPING YOU AND HIM GOING IS NOW AVAILABLE FOR YOU ALONE

GATHER PRAISE

Get together with two or three trusted friends and give everyone a piece of paper. Ask each friend to write her own name at the top and then pass the paper to the person sitting on the left. Each person must write at least 100 words on why the person whose name is on the top of the sheet is so great. Then pass on the pieces of paper again. If it feels awkward, explain that it's part of your campaign to get over your loser. True friends will be glad to help.

START A COMPLIMENT DIARY

Keep a diary or notebook with you at all times and whenever someone says something positive—about the way you look, about your work, about something you've said or done, or just about you—write it down. Read them back often and believe in them!

LET'S PRETEND

Organize a night out with the girls where you give each other permission to be someone completely different. Dress as crazily as you like and let go of your inhibitions. Most of us find it much easier to be confident in borrowed clothes and as a "borrowed" character. At the end of the night, consider how much fun you could have all the time if you acted as confidently as you've just done. After a while, your increased confidence will be more than just an act.

PAMPER YOURSELF

Every magazine you've ever read will have urged you to get over a broken heart by getting a facial, booking a massage, buying yourself a great new outfit. Do you know why they're right? Because if a guy did those things for you you'd feel cherished. Self-esteem is about cherishing yourself.

TALK YOURSELF UP

Write three ads about yourself in your notebook: to find your dream man, your dream roommate, and your dream job. Absolutely no negatives allowed. Your task is to sell yourself—but to do so honestly. Once you've finished, take a look back at what you've written. Aren't you great?

FORGIVE YOURSELF

OK, so you've made some bad choices in love. But you are doing your very best. Every time you want to criticize yourself—for not being able to let go, for something stupid you said or did, for not learning from the past—imagine you're a child again, and the parent looking after her. Cuddle her when she's down, support her through her mistakes, and pick her up when she stumbles.

SOMETHING AS SIMPLE AS TREATING YOURSELF TO A FACIAL, MANICURE, HAIRCUT, PEDICURE, OR NEW OUTFIT CAN HELP BRING YOU BACK ON THE ROAD TO SELF-CONFIDENCE

IT'S ALL ABOUT THE JOURNEY

You probably don't need to be reminded that life moves on and very little ever stays the same. Think back to what you were doing five, ten, or twenty years ago. You've changed, learned, and grown, and it's almost certain that the things that caused you agonies then—lousy grades at school, wearing the wrong brand of shoes, grinning through an interview with spinach in your teeth—do nothing more than raise a knowing smile now.

THE KEY TO BEING A SUCCESSFUL SINGLE IS TO ENJOY EVERY MINUTE OF THE JOURNEY, RATHER THAN FOCUSING ON THE ARRIVAL—BECAUSE THE TRUTH IS WE NEVER REALLY "ARRIVE"

Although you didn't believe it would happen, you've come a long way. So why on earth would you think the world has ended just because your recent relationship has? You may have lost your guy (and remember, he was a loser anyway) but the journey's still on. Indeed, this is where it gets interesting, as you've now stepped off a one-track road, taken the map in your own hands, and can go anywhere, do anything, and be anyone you want to be.

Safe in the knowledge that your life will continue to move on, you can think of going solo as just another

phase in the bigger picture—and one that you should make the most of while you can.

Just imagine you've finally managed to save enough for your vacation of a lifetime. The one you've fantasized about for years. As you step onto your beachside balcony (or out of your tent perched on a mountain top), wouldn't you be determined to squeeze every last moment of experience and enjoyment from the time you've got before you're back at your desk?

Think of this "single" period like that vacation. Who knows? In six months, or six years, you may have found Mr. Right, and the last thing you'd want would be to look back and regret that you didn't make the very most of being young(-ish), free, and single again while you had the chance.

And even when Mr. Right does come along, he shouldn't be the absolute center of your universe. Because that's where you belong—along with all your dreams, goals, and fantasies.

TURNING DREAMS INTO REALITY

The happiest people, the ones we all love to be around, are those with a purpose in life or a dream that they're working to achieve. And while you've been concentrating on your loser, you may have lost sight of these personal goals.

Perhaps you dreamed of a home, husband, and kids, but, being in love with Mr. Married Man, you had to convince yourself it was far cooler to be his mistress than the mistress of your own home. Perhaps you love dancing and envied those friends who signed up for salsa classes, but knew that Mr. Needy wouldn't have been able to cope with you getting up close and personal with other guys. Or maybe your fantasy was that one day you'd leave the rat race and open a small shop selling crafts in the middle of nowhere. But after so many years of being told you're useless by Mr. Controlling, you no longer believe you have the skills to carry it off.

If your aspirations are buried under debris from your losing relationships, think of today as another New Year's Eve. Write down a set of resolutions for the start of a new era in your life, then consider how you can achieve them.

For instance, if you've written down "give up work to become an artist," what's stopping you from going

NOW IS A GREAT TIME TO REDISCOVER YOUR DREAMS AND YOUR PURPOSE—WHO YOU REALLY ARE AND WHAT YOU REALLY WANT—AS YOU'RE NO LONGER PREOCCUPIED WITH TRYING TO BE MS. RIGHT FOR MR. WRONG

to a painting class? If travel tops your list, start saving to buy a round-the-world ticket. Or if having a houseful of animals is what you want, then start off by volunteering to help out at the local shelter.

So many of the things we say we'd do "if given the chance" are actually well within our reach, if only we'd simply be brave enough to stretch out for them. It's not dollars we need to achieve them, it's a can-do attitude, some lateral thinking, and a commitment to working toward our ideal future—even if it has to be step by step rather than in one giant leap.

ENJOYING THE SINGLE LIFE

ALL THOSE TRENDY NEW BARS, CLUBS, RESTAURANTS, AND GYMS—IT'S SINGLE YOU (OK, YOU AND YOUR MONEY) THAT THEY'RE AFTER

Where would hair stylists be if everyone was happy in love? Out of business—because when a relationship ends we often feel like heading straight for a new style.

Cutting that man out of your hair is a great way to start fresh, but why stop there? If he's been cramping your style (or you've been cramping your own style for his sake), this is the time to rediscover all the things you love to do—and some new ones, too.

The first step is to get a notebook and record, hour by hour, everything you do in a week. How much of that time is devoted to things you want to do (like going for long walks), to things you have to do (like working), and to things you think you have to do (like cleaning the shower, visiting relatives, and getting early nights in during the week).

If your "you time" looks like the dregs at the bottom of a bottle, now's the time to get some balance back in your life. Forget what your mom taught you about good girls and housework (at least until she's due a visit) and make your motto "life is for living." Set aside a chunk of time that's all for you every single day of the week. If it helps you to make it happen, adopt a formal approach to doing this by actually scheduling it into your day planner.

As for what to do with that time, you may not need encouragement to switch on the music, pour yourself a glass of wine, and sink into your softest chair with a 600-page blockbuster. Or to pick up the phone and summon your girlfriends for a night on the town.

But don't limit yourself to things you know you enjoy. Think back to what you loved as a child. A two-hour pony trek? Finger-painting? Making up stories for your family? Climbing trees? Dancing naked around the house? Make a list of these things in your notebook and promise yourself you'll do at least one of these activities every week. It's guaranteed you'll have fun and you may even rediscover a hobby or interest you should never have dropped in the first place.

As for that haircut, why stop there? Why not rearrange all the furniture, or revamp your apartment? Learn to cook in a different style or start a new exercise regime?

This is your time and there's every reason to celebrate all the opportunities in store just around the corner.

TIME FOR A CHANGE

You could organize a "wardrobe party" where your closest friends tell you (kindly) which of your clothes suit you and which don't. They can share the "don't" pile among themselves, and you can go to the store with a clear conscience and experiment with new looks to find the desired new you.

CELEBRATING SINGLEDOM

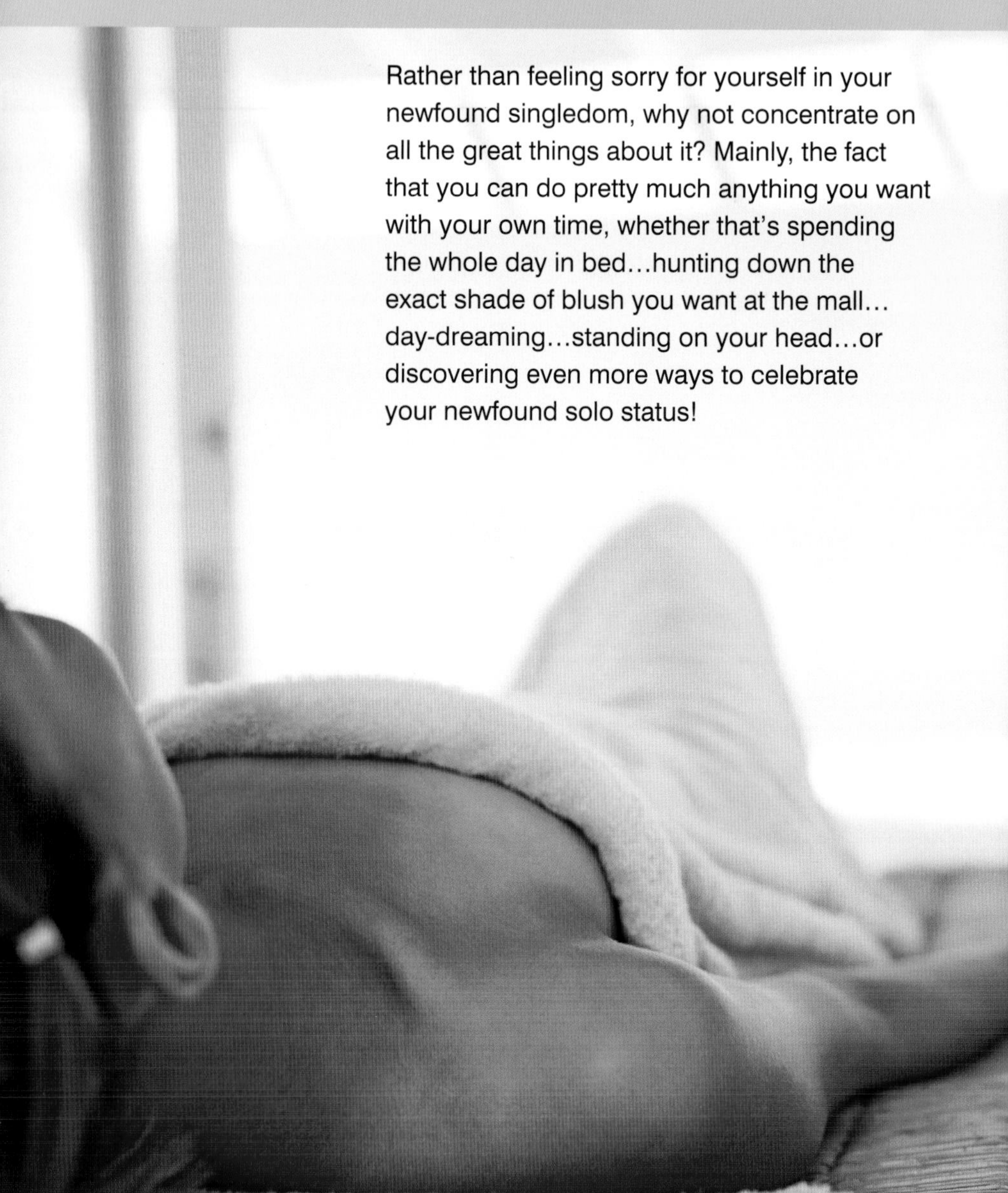

Rather than feeling sorry for yourself in your newfound singledom, why not concentrate on all the great things about it? Mainly, the fact that you can do pretty much anything you want with your own time, whether that's spending the whole day in bed…hunting down the exact shade of blush you want at the mall…day-dreaming…standing on your head…or discovering even more ways to celebrate your newfound solo status!

FOURTEEN FABULOUS REASONS TO CELEBRATE THE SINGLE LIFE

1. You can make plans and jet off any time you like without having to consult anything but your own desire (and bank account of course).
2. No one (other than the cat) cares if there was too much garlic in the pasta sauce.
3. Your phone bill will no longer be enough to bankrupt a small country.
4. You can have all the soft centers in the box of chocolates. In fact, you can have all the chocolates.
5. You can temporarily retire your collection of impractical, lacy underwear in favor of your old comfy set, no matter how faded or unsexy.
6. The toilet seat will never be up and there's no longer a danger of cutting your feet on the toe clippings hidden in the bedroom carpet.
7. It's OK to notice your favorite film star is back on the market (perhaps he heard you were too!).
8. You don't have to have sex—or pretend to want it—when you'd rather have a cup of cocoa.
9. You can wander naked round the house without anyone thinking it's a come on.
10. When you can't sleep, you can raid the fridge and read till dawn without worrying about disturbing him.
11. You no longer have to remember two sets of birthdays and anniversaries or be blamed when he forgets his mom's!
12. You can watch trashy television without having to pretend there's nothing else on.
13. You can go alone to office parties and discover who has secretly liked you for months but couldn't make a move while you were "taken."
14. You can ask girlfriends (or boyfriends for that matter) to your place any time you want, not just on nights when your man's out with his friends.

FAITHFUL FRIENDS

Friends are a crucial part of being a successful single. Because even though you're now alone, alone certainly doesn't mean lonely. Many of the things we look for in a healthy relationship with a guy are equally available from those we call friends: acceptance for who we are; support through thick and thin; knowledge of where we come from and what we're about; as well as all the good-time fun stuff.

Cherish those friendships now, giving and taking from your friends in equal measure. Then, when you do meet the right guy, you won't need him to be everything to you. Plus, having seen you solo, your friends will be perfectly placed to tell you whether he really is the Right Guy when he appears.

It is possible that while you've been with your loser you've become isolated from your friends. Maybe most of the people you saw were "couple friends" and they've now disappeared along with your loser. Or perhaps, with or without a man in your life, you just find it

hard to meet and make new friends. Whatever situation you find yourself in, the company of like-minded people enriches us, so now's the time to make an effort to link up with those in the same situation as you.

PLEASED TO MEET YOU

Meeting and making new friends can be a lot more challenging as we get older and no longer naturally have hundreds of potential like-minded people around us—whether at school, college, or the local youth center. Your place of work is the most likely place for you to meet people, but many people prefer not to mix business with pleasure. There are other places, however, where friends-in-waiting—or even potential partners—may be found (see right).

YOU MAY BE SINGLE BUT TRY NOT TO GIVE UP ON LOVE; SO GET YOURSELF OUT, EVEN IF ONLY TO WINDOW-SHOP

WORTH A VISIT

Health clubs
Men outnumber women at most health clubs, mainly because men are more comfortable bonding with their buddies on exercise bikes than on the bed (like us). OK, so you may not look your best with sweat pouring down your tomato-face, but by the time you're sitting next to him in the juice bar, you'll be glowing.

Singles clubs
Don't dismiss all the dedicated singles clubs springing up, but choose carefully. It's much easier to feel comfortable in a group based on an activity such as dining out or dancing, rather than one where the atmosphere screams "Pick me, pick me!"

Hobby-specific clubs
And what about all the other clubs and groups just waiting to welcome you? If it's male company you're after, you may prefer to join the local sailing or scuba diving club than the sewing class. But if sewing's your thing, do it anyway. There will be women there who share your passion and new friends will introduce you to new places and even new faces.

Organized vacations
Take a trip based on something you love to do: Tai Chi, touring classical Egypt, or wine-tasting. It's almost impossible not to make new friends in a group of people with shared interests.

Volunteer work
Sign up as a volunteer in an area which interests you—children, politics, the environment. Wouldn't it be fantastic to meet a potential partner who loves doing similar things as you?

DEALING WITH THE BLUES

Just because you're off the emotional roller coaster doesn't mean you won't have the occasional bad day. And remember, so does everyone else. It may be related to your feelings about your relationships. But it may equally be about hormones, gray skies, the unfeasibly large phone bill, or any of the other daily details we all live with. It's important when you have down days to be honest with yourself about what's behind them, especially if you find yourself thinking about your now ex.

Another important thing is to be honest about where the rest of the world is at. It's very tempting when you're down to think everyone else is ten times more together than you and having a great time. Or that the whole world is made up of couples and that you're left looking over the fence—along with all the other losers—seeing how happy they are compared to poor you.

But it's not all couples and they're not always happy. Look at the problem page in every glossy magazine. Look at the tortuous relationships of the rich and famous. Think about how you looked when you were with your loser. Did you dash around with a big board over your heads proclaiming how unhappy you both were? Or did your break-up come as a surprise to some because you always looked as though you were OK?

Every seemingly successful couple you see has times when they don't like each other very much, when they have to work at understanding each other and growing together. And there's a very good chance that many of those you see also worked their way through a lot of losers before they learned to be winners in love.

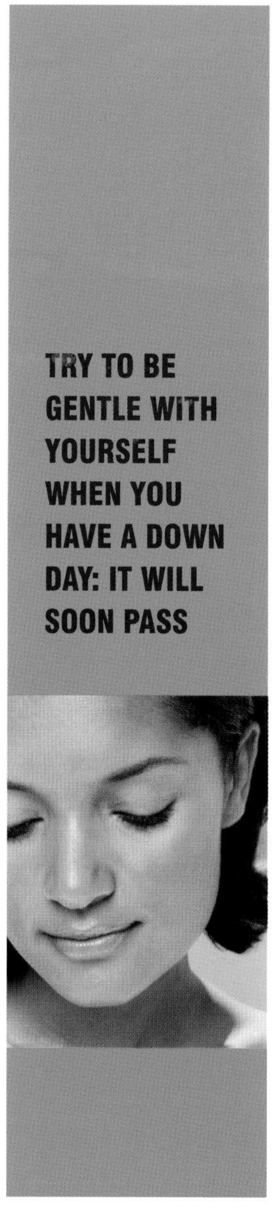

If you decide that your situation is more than just the occasional "down day," it's possible that you still haven't properly worked through all the stages of your loss. Having a few sessions of counseling is a good way of dealing with feeling stuck in this rut and could help you discover what's holding you back. Even if you feel you're coping fairly well, you might want to get some professional help—just to make sure you really are heading toward the brighter future you deserve.

Just bear in mind that bad days are inevitable. Look at the list of emotionally "dangerous" situations on the following page for ideas on how you can negotiate your way through them.

EMOTIONAL ALERT!

No matter how well you're coping with your break-up, you're still likely to find yourself in the odd upsetting situation, such as those that follow.

It's Valentine's Day, your colleagues are vying for the "Who got the most cards" title, and taxis seem to be outnumbered by florists' vans delivering what seems like thousands of red roses into homes and offices across the country. But you haven't got one. Boo hoo.

Scour the shops for Valentine's cards with loving messages to send to all those fantastic people who have supported you through your break-up. Who says romantic love is the only game in town? And order a massive cheer-up bouquet to be delivered anonymously to your own desk.

A relative asks about your loser and says what a nice guy he is and how well suited you two are. No need to defend your decision to ditch him. But you might want to drop into the conversation that the thing you hated most about him was the way he trashed your relatives behind their backs.

YOU KNOW YOU DID THE RIGHT THING IN LOSING HIM—JUST KEEP TELLING YOURSELF SO

Your well-meaning buddy invites you to "even up the numbers" at a dinner party where everyone else is in a couple apart from another "newly single" (male) who just happens to be sitting next to you. At all costs avoid getting drawn into any losers-in-love conversation: your role now is sassy solo, not sorrowful saddo. Remind yourself, and the guy sitting next to you, that there's a good chance half of the couples round the table actually envy you (it's true!).

Your mates drag you to a new chickflick where you disgrace yourself by weeping into your popcorn throughout.

There's more than one way to wash him out of your system: tears are wonderfully therapeutic so cry away, make sure you have plenty of tissues, and tell your friends they've simply got no soul.

Everyone's planning their summer vacation and you're sad that there's no one for you to snuggle up with in the sand under a silver moon in some seaside town.

This is the year to sign up for an activity vacation, whether you choose to learn yoga in Mexico, sail a boat around the Greek islands, or go sheep-shearing in Australia. You still get the sun, sea, and souvenirs, but you also get the stimulation of doing something different and the security of being with people who will almost all have come alone, too.

You're in a store and suddenly realize they're playing *All by Myself*, or worse—"your tune." Make a dash for the exit, race home, and put on *I Will Survive*, *Sisters are Doing It for Themselves*, or the theme from *The Great Escape*. Declare your home a ballad-free zone—for now at least.

You hear through the grapevine that your ex has not only met someone, but they've gotten engaged. How foolish of him for missing out on the joys of going solo for a while, and her for hooking up with someone so obviously on the rebound. Head for the basketball or tennis court with a friend to channel your mixed feelings into action involving a different kind of rebound.

NO MORE LOSERS

Once you have taken control of and also responsibility for your own life and happiness, you will not only gain confidence, but also a great deal of inner strength.

Remember when the time comes to put yourself back on the market for a man, you're not looking for someone to complete you. If you've explored being single properly, you'll be complete within yourself, which means you can search for someone to complement you, rather than plug the gaps in your life and personality.

The fact that you enjoy the single life doesn't mean you don't want intimacy, supportive relationships, and for a Mr. Right to whisk you off your feet. But you're learning that these things aren't essential to your survival. You not only can cope alone, you can actually thrive. And this makes you infinitely more desirable to the type of guy you'd want to build a healthy relationship with, as well as very off-putting to any loser who chances to come your way.

You won't care that Mr. Theoretically Gorgeous is also Mr. Unavailable, because in your eyes that makes him plain Undesirable and Unattractive in the first place. And if Mr. Bad Boy can only offer to warm your bed once in a while, you'll just stick to the

THE SELF-AWARE, SELF-ASSURED, INDEPENDENT YOU WILL ATTRACT A WINNING BREED OF GUYS

electric blanket instead (it has never once asked you to praise its abilities and then not called the next day). As for Mr. Unreliable, why bother with him when you have half a dozen good friends—both male and female—who you can count on, as well as being able to fall back on the new, resourceful you, of course! You finally realize that being on your own can be much more fun than being with Mr. Wrong for the sake of it.

GREAT NEWS: YOU HAVEN'T ONLY LOST YOUR LOSER—YOU SHOULD HAVE LOST YOUR TASTE FOR FUTURE LOSERS IN THE PROCESS

CHAPTER 6

FINDING A NEW MAN

How many times have you scoured the stores in vain looking for shoes that exactly match your new dress, and then stumbled on them months after you stopped looking?

You'll find it works exactly the same in the game of love. Once you've reached the point of being a satisfied single who knows the difference between needing and wanting a guy, Mr. Right will show up sooner or later—just like those shoes.

Just remember everything you've learned to ensure that the "new shoes" you buy are a good fit—rather than something that will once again seriously cramp your style.

REALITY CHECK

The following exercise is a great way to help you decide whether you're really ready for a successful new relationship.

ONLY START THINKING ABOUT GETTING TOGETHER WITH ANOTHER GUY WHEN YOU DON'T MIND IF HE TAKES HIS TIME TURNING UP

Write down all the reasons you'd like a guy in your life again. How do you think being with a guy again would improve your life? Now look hard at your list. Does it include the elements of a healthy relationship that enhances the lives of both partners equally?

- To love, laugh, and learn alongside.
- To support and be supported.
- To have a companion and new best friend.
- To share dreams, desires, and fears with.
- For a warm (or wild) sex life—whatever your taste.

TWO HALVES = WHOLE?

Usually two halves make a whole, but when it comes to relationships, two halves simply remain two halves—like two left shoes, they just make moving more awkward. So, only when you feel whole by yourself and know you can survive perfectly well alone (but would love to continue the journey with another survivor at your side), are you really ready for a new relationship.

IF YOU DON'T FEEL YOU'RE GETTING OVER YOUR BREAK-UP, YOU MAY WANT TO JOIN A SELF-ESTEEM CLASS

Or have some of the negative discoveries you made about yourself in chapter 2 raised their unwelcome, stubborn heads again?

- Your need to be needed by someone.
- Your desire for someone to take charge of your life for you.
- Your search for a better reason to get up in the morning.
- Your desire for someone else to patch the roof or fix your car.

If so, you still need to spend a little more time getting to know and like yourself. It may be worth seeking the help of a counselor to support you.

ARE YOU READY FOR LOVE?

You've come this far, but have you really washed that loser out of your hair or do traces of him still linger, like dandruff on your collar? The following quiz is a useful way to check for sure, so be honest with yourself as you do it.

DESCRIBE YOUR LIFE AS A SINGLE

a) I enjoy my own company and I'm having fun but it would be nicer to have someone to share things with.
b) Being alone gives me too much time to think about where I've been going wrong—it's odd the way people never seem to be in when I call to talk about it.
c) I've just had "Women need men like chickens need sunbeds" tattooed on my back.

HOW DO YOU FEEL WHEN YOU THINK ABOUT HIM AND YOUR TIME TOGETHER?

a) Sad and a little wistful but also older and wiser. I learned a lot from the experience.
b) Sometimes I'm angry with him and with myself for putting up with him; other times I think it wasn't so bad and that maybe I should have given him one more chance.
c) Loser? What loser?

HOW OFTEN DO YOU NOW TALK ABOUT YOUR LOSER TO YOUR FRIENDS—HONESTLY?

a) His name comes up from time to time.

b) Honestly? We're always talking about him but I'm sure it's my friends who bring the subject up.

c) I still don't know what you're talking about!

YOU'RE IN A BAR AND A FRIENDLY-LOOKING GUY PAYS YOU A COMPLIMENT AND ASKS FOR YOUR NUMBER. HOW DO YOU REACT?

a) Hmm. I suggest he gives me his number instead as I'm often hard to get hold of.

b) Give him my cell, office line, email address, and postal address, plus instructions of when he can reach me on each one.

c) OK, he's well-disguised but beneath that tasty exterior he's almost certain to have loser tendencies, so I smile and turn away.

YOU'LL ONLY BE READY FOR LOVE AGAIN WHEN YOU'RE SECURE ENOUGH TO KNOW THAT NOT HAVING A GUY DOESN'T DIMINISH YOU, OR THE LIFE YOU'RE LIVING

HOW DID YOU SCORE?

It's time to face up to the truth about whether you're over him or not.

Mostly a's: Your feet are well-planted on the ground and you're using them to move on. You've learned about yourself and are embracing change. Go on. Give that new guy a ring. What have you got to lose?	Mostly b's: Your feet may be on the ground but they're encased in concrete Ms. Desperate. You should turn quickly on your heels and retrace your steps back through the pages of this book.	Mostly c's: Are you sure you're not just protecting yourself from any more hurt by writing off half the human race? You had better examine where you really stand before you become any more bitter.

THE SHOPPING LIST APPROACH

Have you ever been warned not to go shopping when you're hungry—because you usually spend a fortune, only to find there's nothing in your basket you can actually turn into a meal.

WHAT ARE THE ESSENTIAL MALE INGREDIENTS TO SATISFY YOUR APPETITE FOR LOVE AND CONTENTMENT?

Well, the same principle could easily be said to apply when "shopping" for a new relationship. The moment you start to fall for a new guy, hunger is pretty likely to take over. One minute you don't know his name, the next you know his shoe size, where he was born, and whether he still has his appendix or not. You invent reasons to bring him into every conversation; drive to work using the route that goes past his place on the offchance of seeing him; save up everything that happens to you to tell him about later; and your heart (or some other organ a little lower down) goes into

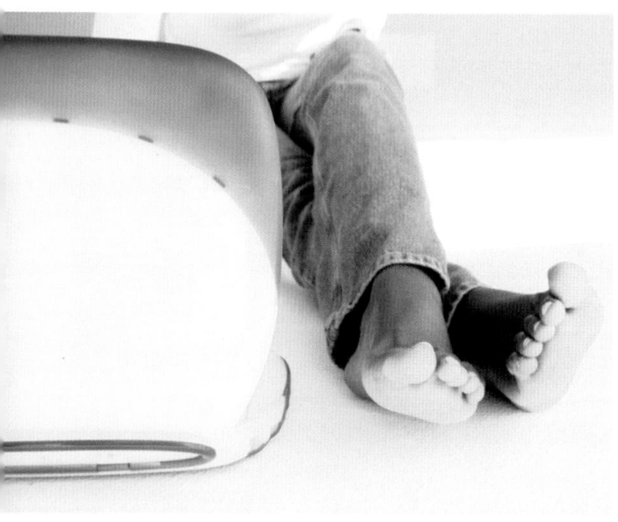

WHILE WRITING YOUR SHOPPING LIST, LOOK BACK TO THE EXERCISE ABOUT YOUR PAST RELATIONSHIPS (SEE PP. 36–37). ARE THERE ANY OTHER QUALITIES THAT YOU CONSIDER ESSENTIAL TO A POTENTIAL MR. RIGHT?

overdrive every time the phone rings or you get a text message.

There's nothing wrong with being in the first flush of love (and lust). It's one of those times when life moves up a gear and you live each day in glorious Technicolor. Enjoy it while it lasts, but don't forget that while you're operating almost entirely at the level of your delighted emotions, the voices of good sense, judgment, experience, and all those other positive qualities you've been busy developing will struggle to be heard above the noise of dramatic drum rolls and heavenly choirs.

This means there's just a tiny chance you could get it wrong for yourself again, and end up with yet another loser. So long before you get to the stage of being in the grip of this overwhelming hunger for Mr. Right, set aside some time for yourself and write a shopping list of the qualities you would like your future partner to have.

Promise yourself no matter how tasty he is, you won't give in to the temptation to vary any of the truly essential ingredients of your recipe. See overleaf to remind yourself of some of the standard men-basics.

GREAT THINGS ABOUT GREAT GUYS

One girl's loser often turns out to be another girl's winner, but some qualities are likely to feature on most girls' (and guys') list.

MR. RIGHT IS UNLIKELY TO TURN UP ON A WHITE HORSE, SO HERE'S SOME TIPS TO HELP YOU RECOGNIZE HIM WHEN HE DOES ARRIVE

Mr. Right:

- Knows he's not perfect (he might have a flatpack rather than a six-pack) but is happy within himself.
- Has a few close friends, a wider group he socializes with, and is in touch with a couple of his ex-girlfriends.
- Has read *Men are from Mars, Women are from Venus* but says that still leaves several other planets where the sexes can meet and try to get it right.
- Doesn't change the subject when you want to talk about "your relationship" even if he shuffles about in the chair a bit.
- Openly demonstrates his affection for you, whether you're making an obligatory visit to family or making out at home (hopefully he'll demonstrate it in a slightly different way).
- Loves to make you laugh, hates to make you cry, is willing to make you breakfast in bed.
- Is generous—with his time, attention, and money—but also sets sensible limits for himself and his resources,

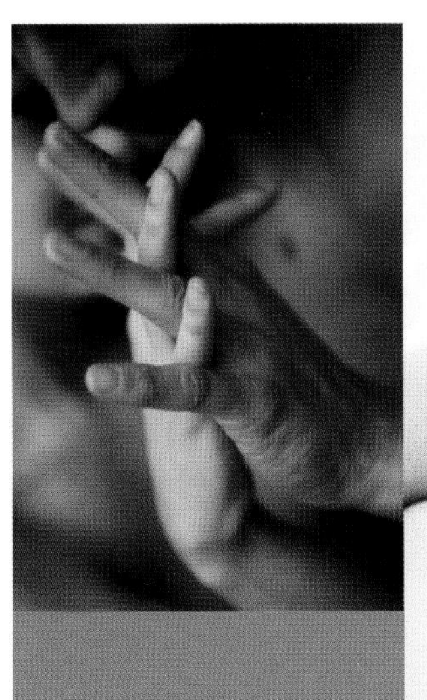

ANY GREAT GUY WILL KNOW AND RECOGNIZE HIS OWN STRENGTHS AND WEAKNESSES

based on having solid self-esteem.

- Is strong enough to be able to show his weaknesses: he'll investigate the late-night noises if you get rid of the spider in the corner.
- Understands that intimacy is not just a polite word for sex, but is about addressing the needs and wants of both partners.

ADDED EXTRAS

What else have you learned about factors that will add to your overall happiness? Will it take more than just the essential ingredients to rock your long-term boat?

Perhaps you're so certain you want marriage and children there's no point spending time getting to know someone who never will. Perhaps you're determined he won't be Mr. Right unless he shares your social or cultural background—or even your passion for dressing up as a character from "Star Trek." Or you know yourself well enough to recognize you'll never be happy with a guy who eats meat, doesn't earn a good wage, or can't make the earth move (or at least quiver a bit) in bed.

On the other hand, it may be that beyond a few essentials concerning who he is and how he behaves, you couldn't care less whether he's tall, short, skinny, or from the planet Zog. Differences can make for compatibility just as much as having things in common.

Neither approach is right or wrong. What you write is a reflection of all the growing and learning you've done—and your commitment to losing your loser and finding and building the best relationship for you and your partner-to-be.

THE ONLY MEASURE OF WHAT YOU PUT ON YOUR MR. RIGHT SHOPPING LIST IS WHAT'S RIGHT FOR YOU AND YOU ALONE

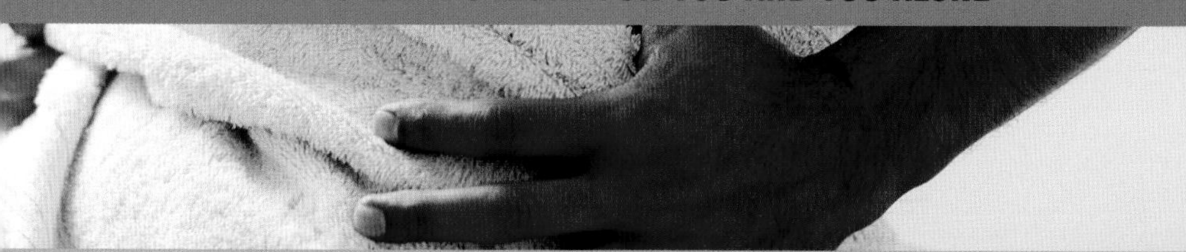

BLIND-SIDED BY MR. RIGHT

A couple of notes of caution. The first is that the guys you meet have every right to be just as specific about what works for them as you do.

IN THE END, THE ONLY TRUE MR. RIGHT IS THE ONE WHO'S LOOKING FOR THE SAME TYPE OF RELATIONSHIP AS YOU

And don't expect to discover whether you've met your match right away. Unless he's obliging enough to arrive on your doorstep with his CV (or you place your own lonely hearts ad specifying precisely who should, or should not, apply—in which case, good luck to you), then your first conversations are unlikely to start "So if this works out, will you marry me?" Just keep your "shopping list" in mind and keep checking out the relationship and how it makes you feel.

You very probably won't find your Mr. Right right away, but you've come so far that it should be a whole lot more fun looking for him this time around.

The final note of caution concerns Elena who featured in the very first chapter with her fatal attraction for Mr. Married Man. After so many years limping from one married loser to another, her friends never thought she'd ever wean herself off her addiction to men who couldn't stay the night, meet her family, take her on vacation, show her in public,

or even wipe her nose when she was sick. It took four years of her feeling hurt, angry, abandoned, desolate, bitter, and sad, but also taking up yoga, volunteering with a charity, and retraining as an adult education teacher before she was really ready to move on. She finally met her Mr. Right in one of her classes. What is interesting, however, is that she failed to notice him at first, because he was in disguise.

With disbelief in her voice Elena says: "He maintains he came up on my blind side. All these years I've been looking for Mr. Right in a certain kind of body. George is nothing like any guy I've ever been with. He's a lot older for one thing and has never bothered about trying to be fit—or even look fit! But he's also intelligent, sexy, funny, genuine, and he adores me. I feel as if I don't have to be anyone but myself when I'm with him. I didn't expect love to be like this."

So bear in mind: you never know where Mr. Right will pop up.

TUNE IN TO YOUR FEELINGS

You may well have been stuck in a needy rut when with your loser, but your life was fueled by emotion. And even though those emotions were negative ones, like insecurity, anger, or frustration, they brought an edginess, a perverse excitement to the relationship. Don't make the mistake of thinking it's not love just because that adrenaline is missing, or because it seems too easy or too peaceful to be what you've been looking for all this time.

There's another area where you need to trust your deepest instincts and that's when it comes to knowing the difference between Mr. Wrong, Mr. Right, and Mr. Right Direction.

A healthy level of self-esteem gives you the confidence to not only hold out for what you want from love, but to trust the tools you have within you to help you get it. He may not be a loser but he still may not be right for you, so trust your intuition and remember you have the right to say "no."

Paying attention to your instincts also means being alert to the warning bells that ring in your head the first time your new man does any of the following:

- Holds back something obvious like where he lives, his phone number, or his email.

BEWARE OF MISSING WHAT YOU'RE LOOKING FOR BECAUSE IT DOESN'T ARRIVE WITH A FANFARE

- Scares you with the strength of his feelings at an early stage.
- Puts you down and you sense it was deliberate.
- Generally pays too much attention to other women.
- Lies to you.

Also stay alert to the first time you have to compromise your own personality, beliefs, or values to suit him and his ways.

Remember you have just been brave enough to bid a final farewell to Mr. Bad Boy, Married Man, Needy, Unreliable, and the rest of the loser gang. They may still need you, but you definitely don't need them any more.

Finally, get to know the difference between instinct and feelings associated with your past. However well you now understand yourself and your past, the baggage will always lurk in your attic. Watch out for feelings which seem too strong for the situation and give yourself the space to work out whether it's your intuition—or the past—calling.

COME IN MR. RIGHT

There is endless advice around on where to meet your Mr. Right—many of which you'll already be trying thanks to your desire to be a satisfied single.

On a planet of several billion people, there's no shortage of potential partners waiting to meet you so long as you make the effort to put yourself in their path, whether through single groups, parties, dating agencies, small ads, internet chat rooms, social clubs, blind dates, or work conferences.

And don't be put off by horror stories about certain methods any more than allow yourself to be seduced by heavily embellished stories of sweet success. For every person who would never dream of trying to build a relationship screen to screen rather than face to face, someone else is now sharing living space with someone they met in cyberspace. After all, you may have been out of the dating game for some time and not just forgotten the moves, but be unaware of the means. Lonely hearts ads—once seen as the territory of the sad or seedy—are now as mainstream as advertising your car or home; and many a happy relationship started with a text message.

After all the work you've done on yourself, it's good to keep pushing your own boundaries back a little every now and then, so be prepared for a

FIND WAYS OF MEETING PEOPLE THAT WORK WELL FOR YOU, BUT ALSO EXPERIMENT WITH METHODS THAT TAKE YOU OUTSIDE YOUR COMFORT ZONE

certain amount of unease as you venture out into the dating game again. But also be aware of the difference between discomfort and pain. If you join a singles dinner club to make new friends of both sexes but sense that the only course everyone else is interested in is intercourse, make your excuses and leave.

If your methods of getting out there start to hurt or bring you out in night sweats, you're not respecting your own boundaries and it's simply not worth it.

GENTLY DOES IT

He's lovely, he wants the same things as you, and you've known almost from the moment he first opened his mouth that your relationship would be an important one.

REMIND YOURSELF THAT IF IT'S RIGHT IT WON'T STOP BEING RIGHT JUST BECAUSE YOU BOTH TAKE YOUR TIME

That's fantastic. Enjoy those feelings and the fun of getting to know him. But don't feel you have to rush into anything before you—and just as importantly, he—are really ready.

When everything feels right, it's tempting to skip a few of the getting-to-know-you stages, to go from "How are you?" straight to "How do you like your breakfast eggs cooked?" because you're clear about what you want, so feel certain about him. But remember that unless he's equally certain about you from the start, your haste could scare him off. After all, unless you really have found a guy from the planet Zog, he'll be lugging some baggage behind him, too. You need to be aware and sensitive to what could be happening on his blindside.

And think hard about when you're ready for sex again. You may be missing it and so much in lust that it's hard to resist wanting to bundle him into your bed at the first opportunity. But remember that for many of

us, moving the relationship on to a physical footing is a signal it has deepened and strengthened, while for others it's not. Sex and intimacy aren't necessarily the same thing, so wait till you're sure making love will be an equal rather than a one-sided experience.

BUILD YOUR OWN FUTURE

We've learned from almost every magazine or book we've ever read that real-life relationships require work, which—with the best will in the world—is not what we always want to hear as we struggle to juggle all the other bits of our lives.

Work equals effort, which equals both time and energy—the two things in shortest supply in many people's lives. A part of us has always thought of love as a refuge, the place we escape to when we're tired of trying to be a complete success in every other area of life.

But there are many kinds of refuge, and what you create with Mr. Right is entirely up to you both. There is all the difference in the world between laying one brick on top of another every day of your life, and designing and creating the amazing building you've always dreamed of living in. One is just back-breaking hard work; while the other is an act requiring creativity, commitment, patience, collaboration, communication, courage, and belief in your partner and yourself. It's not just work for the sake of work, it's actually a work of art, and the rewards for both of you are enormous.

You get to go on growing, learning about yourself and about him, to live your life as an adventure in which it's possible to make your dreams come true.

With Mr. Right by your side—whoever he turns out to be, and whichever side he sneaks up on you

IT'S ONLY IN FAIRY TALES THAT RELATIONSHIPS START WITH THE FIRST KISS AND END HAPPILY EVER AFTER

from—you'll achieve even more than you can alone. With your winning relationship providing the foundations, you can build a future which offers more richness, excitement, stability, fulfillment, and opportunities—whatever it is you seek—than you ever imagined.

So no more losers ever again. Just the right guy and the right relationship at the right time. Right?

INDEX

Acknowledgments

Thanks to Jackie Ruane for casting an expert eye over the text, sharing her experience, and making some helpful suggestions for improvements.